TIME

1989
The Year That Defined
Today's World

THE EDGE OF AN ERA *A German straddles the Berlin Wall on Nov. 11, 1989*

TIME

MANAGING EDITOR Richard Stengel
ART DIRECTOR Arthur Hochstein

1989
The Year That Defined Today's World

EDITOR Michael Elliott
INTERNATIONAL ART DIRECTOR Cecelia Wong
PICTURE EDITOR Maria Wood
SENIOR EDITORS Zoher Abdoolcarim, Jim Erickson, Charlotte Greensit, Simon Robinson
ASSOCIATE ART DIRECTOR May Wong
DEPUTY PICTURE EDITOR Christie Johnston
REPORTER Andréa Ford
EDITORIAL PRODUCTION Henry Ho
COPY EDITORS Vanessa Harriss, Tim Youngs

TIME INC. HOME ENTERTAINMENT

PUBLISHER Richard Fraiman
GENERAL MANAGER Steven Sandonato
EXECUTIVE DIRECTOR, MARKETING SERVICES Carol Pittard
DIRECTOR, RETAIL & SPECIAL SALES Tom Mifsud
DIRECTOR, NEW PRODUCT DEVELOPMENT Peter Harper
ASSISTANT DIRECTOR, NEWSSTAND MARKETING Laura Adam
ASSISTANT DIRECTOR, BRAND MARKETING Joy Butts
ASSOCIATE COUNSEL Helen Wan
BOOK PRODUCTION MANAGER Suzanne Janso
DESIGN & PREPRESS MANAGER Anne-Michelle Gallero
ASSOCIATE BRAND MANAGER Michela Wilde

SPECIAL THANKS TO:
Christine Austin, Glenn Buonocore, Jim Childs, Susan Chodakiewicz, Rose Cirrincione, Jacqueline Fitzgerald, Lauren Hall, Jennifer Jacobs, Brynn Joyce, Mona Li, Robert Marasco, Amy Migliaccio, Brooke Reger, Dave Rozzelle, Ilene Schreider, Adriana Tierno, Alex Voznesenskiy, Sydney Webber

Copyright © 2009 Time Inc. Home Entertainment
Published by TIME Books, Time Inc. • 1271 Avenue of the Americas • New York, NY 10020

ISBN 10: 1-60320-133-5
ISBN 13: 978-1-60320-133-9
Library of Congress Number: 2009936240

We welcome your comments and suggestions about TIME Books. Please write to us at:
TIME Books, Attention: Book Editors, P.O. Box 11016, Des Moines, IA 50336-1016

If you would like to order any of our hardcover Collector's Edition books, please call us at 1-800-327-6388 (Monday through Friday, 7:00 a.m.— 8:00 p.m., or Saturday, 7:00 a.m.— 6:00 p.m., Central Time).

STEVE LISS—TIME & LIFE PICTURES/GETTY

INAUGURATION DAY *With the world on the verge of great change, Reagan leaves his successor, Bush, at the helm*

SEA CHANGE *During the velvet revolution,*
Czechoslovakians pack the streets of Prague

Contents

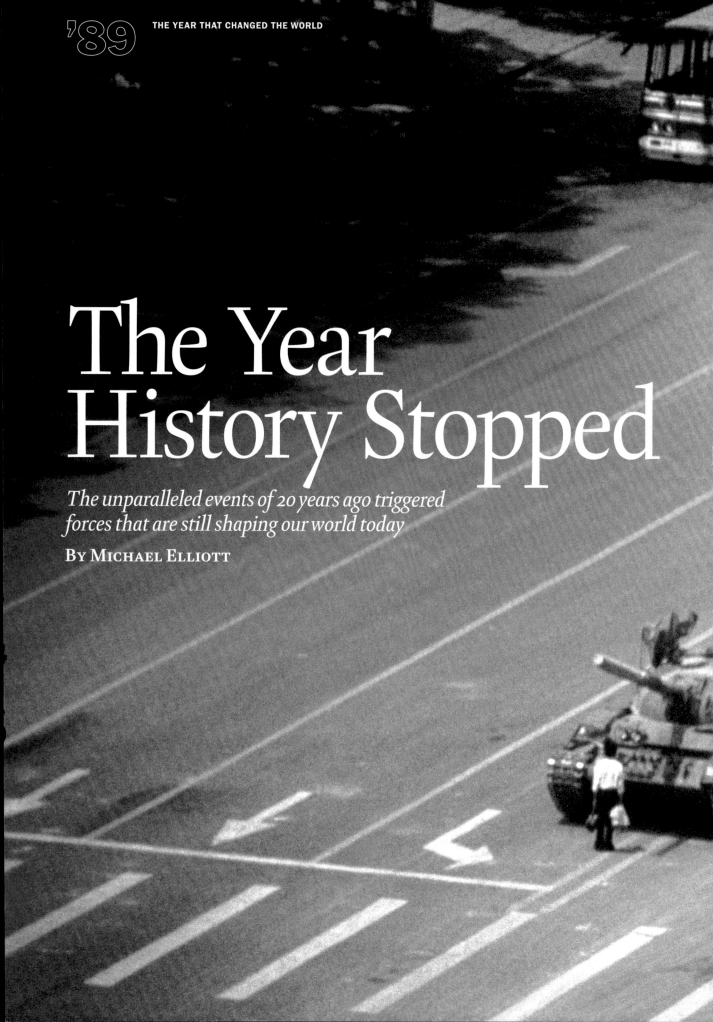

The Year History Stopped

The unparalleled events of 20 years ago triggered forces that are still shaping our world today

BY MICHAEL ELLIOTT

STANDSTILL *An unknown Beijing man blocks tanks the day after many were killed in and around Tiananmen*

I F YOU THINK YOU'RE SOMETIMES spoiled for choice, consider the lot of a news editor on the first weekend of June 1989. On the afternoon of Saturday, June 3, the condition of Ayatullah Ruhollah Khomeini, the Supreme Leader of Iran, began to rapidly deteriorate. Just before midnight, Khomeini, 86, died; his death was announced on the radio a few hours later. Tehran is 3½ hours behind Beijing, so at just the time crowds in Iran were taking to the streets in extraordinary expressions of grief, the people of Beijing, no less in shock, were coming to terms with what had happened in the early hours of that Sunday morning. Troops of the People's Liberation Army had cleared the remnants of student protests in Tiananmen Square, shooting into the crowds as they did so.

But that was not all. As grief and horror respectively gripped Tehran and Beijing, Poles were awakening to a day of hope. In the spring, in the opening steps of a dance that would captivate the world, Poland's ruling Communist Party had been compelled to open roundtable talks with the opposition, including representatives of Solidarity, the civic and trade-union group that had survived the imposition of martial law in 1981. In Hungary in 1956, and again in Czechoslovakia in 1968, Soviet tanks had crushed popular reform movements. By 1989, however, the winds of change in Eastern Europe had reached gale force. In the Soviet Union itself, the General Secretary of the Communist Party, Mikhail Gorbachev, was discarding old habits like a teenager throwing out last year's fashions. The Soviet leadership no longer had the stony heart or iron fist to impose its rule by force of arms. And so on June 4, Poland was to hold an election. When the two rounds of

By 1989, all but the most calcified communist leaders knew that at the most practical level—providing a decent standard of living to their people—their god had failed

votes were counted, Solidarity had won virtually every seat in the Sejm, Poland's parliament, that it could contest. The division that had scarred Europe since the end of World War II was coming to an end. The rivets in the Iron Curtain were beginning to pop.

All Changed

HISTORIANS, PICKING OVER WHAT HAS gone before, revising past judgments, will tell you that our understanding of the past is never final. What were thought to be world-changing events dim into topics of an obscure Ph.D. thesis; what seemed to be small stories turn out to be the ones that shaped the future. All is relative.

Yet 1989 truly was one of those years in which the world shifted on its pivot. Some things did change, and changed utterly; we are living with their consequences still. Some things ended too—not just the Cold War, for example, but also the idea that the international system is driven solely by the actions of states. In a way that was only dimly perceived 20 years ago, multinational business, technological innovation and personal faith now shape our world just as states do.

1989's significance was understood at the time. In the most famous contemporary analysis of current events, Francis Fukuyama, a brilliant American scholar who was then serving on the policy-planning staff of the U.S. State Department, published an essay in the *National Interest,* a small Washington journal, entitled "The End of History." The statement of his central thesis was unequivocal: "What we may be witnessing is not just the end of the Cold War, or the passing of a particular period of postwar history, but the end of history as such: that is, the end point

**UNDER
PRESSURE**
*Soldiers near
Tiananmen
Square during
pro-democracy
protests*

of mankind's ideological evolution and the universalization of Western liberal democracy as the final form of human government."

In history's hourglass, 20 years amounts to just a dribble of sand. Despite the criticism heaped on them, it is still too early to know if Fukuyama's claims will be fully borne out. But one aspect of Fukuyama's thesis has been proved right in spades. Notwithstanding the fact that in 2008-09 the world economy suffered the most severe contraction in 70 years, there really has been "an unabashed victory of economic liberalism" over a competing economic system—that of a centrally planned economy—which once appeared to offer an alternative to free markets.

By 1989, all but the most calcified leaders in the communist world knew that at the most practical level—providing a decent standard of living to their people—their god had failed. The blustery claims that planned economies would bury the West had been silenced. In the U.S., a revolution in information and communication technology had spread from giant corporations through the garages and bedrooms of Silicon Valley, until once unimaginable computing power was placed in the hands of individual consumers. As America's passion for risk-taking became fueled by easy access to capital—and as the products and habits of innovation spread to Japan and Western Europe—so the Eastern bloc got left behind. Surveying the pinched, stunted lives their people lived and the stores filled (and hardly that) with shoddy goods, Soviet leaders such as Gorbachev and Aleksandr Yakovlev, who had spent 10 years in Canada, knew that capitalism had won.

It was not just the European communists who had come to that conclusion. So did those in China. Fukuyama noted that "anyone familiar with the outlook and behavior of the new technocratic élite now governing China knows that Marxism and ideological principle have become virtually irrelevant as guides to policy, and that bourgeois consumerism has a real meaning in that country for the first time since the revolution." In the journals, released this year, of Zhao Ziyang, an economic reformer who rose to become General Secretary of the Chinese Communist Party before being ousted just before the Tiananmen massacre, there is a marvelous passage on the wonders of free trade. Zhao lamented that in Mao Zedong's China, "self-reliance"

was "an absolute virtue. It became an ideological pursuit and was politicized." Only after reform, he continued, "could we take advantage of what we had, and trade for what we needed." David Ricardo could not have put it better.

The broad consensus that free markets and free trade are the surest route to dispersed prosperity has survived the many modern crises of capitalism. Not even the Great Recession has persuaded people to throw over the market system. To be sure, from the U.S. to China, policy responses to the economic crisis have contemplated an increased role for the state. But there

AFTER THE FALL *The end of the Berlin Wall opened the door for a reunified Germany*

is an intellectual chasm between Keynesian stimulus packages, on the one hand, and the assumption that the state can and should plan the economy on the other. Those who doubt it, and who think that the world (including the U.S.!) is going socialist, are too young to remember the sheer audacity of those who once thought that economies could be planned, or the miserable consequences of their belief.

Europe's Glory Lost

ONE CONSEQUENCE OF THE COMMON POL-icy response to the economic crisis has been the realization that, as UCLA professor Peter Baldwin put it in *Prospect* magazine, the Atlantic is narrower than many have assumed. There are of course differences in European and American views of the world, especially in their attitudes to the use of force as a policy tool. For many Americans, the historian Tony Judt has written, "the message of the last century is that war works." With memories of their bloodstained recent past still fresh, few Europeans now think that. George W. Bush, with a Texan swagger and the conviction of the born-again that God was on his and his nation's side, was distinctly unappealing to

IRAN IN MOURNING *Crowds gather in grief after the death of Ayatullah Ruhollah Khomeini*

JEAN GAUMY—MAGNUM PHOTOS

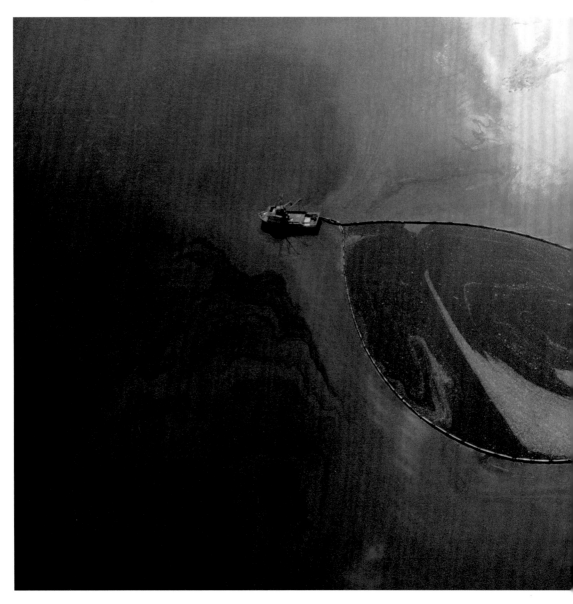

CATASTROPHE
A fish trawler uses a net to gather crude oil spillled in Prince William Sound, Alaska

Europeans. But Bush is no longer President; Barack Obama is, and anyone who can get 200,000 cheering Germans into the streets is someone with whom Europeans are happy to see their future linked.

It's worth remembering: both Europe and the U.S. are democratic, capitalist and open societies. Contrary to the European idea that the U.S. is a place where the devil takes the hindmost, nations on both sides of the Atlantic value substantial social safety nets. "The American welfare state is more extensive than is often realized," writes Baldwin. Many Europeans have

rejoiced in the policies that the Obama Administration has taken during the financial crisis. In its determination to control the excesses of financial markets, the U.S. can now seem almost Scandinavian in its commitment to a sort of duvet capitalism, warm and fuzzy. It's enough to make Europeans think—as some have insisted since 1989—that when it comes to the power of example in the world, it is Europe, with its combination of free markets and social protection, rather than the U.S., that will lead the way.

It is a comforting thought, but it cuts no ice. Paradoxically, 1989, that year when Europe

LARRY TOWELL—MAGNUM PHOTOS

14

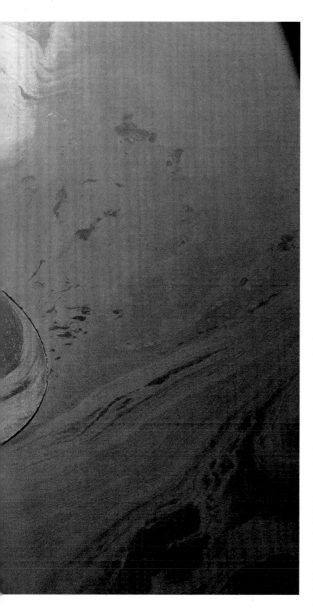

it is a failure. Far from it; the two decades since 1989 have been a golden age in Europe, which has become the most extensive space of peace and widely shared prosperity in the world. As Europeans have become used to the gentlemanly negotiations and compromises that typify life in the European Union—now with 27 members, when it had just 12 in 1989—so the old nationalism, which twice in the last century dragged the whole world into Europe's arguments, has died away. In its place has come what might be called "football nationalism"—the waving of national flags and full-throated singing of national anthems done not to send young men off to war, but to cheer them on in sports stadiums. In many ways, Europe today represents a wonderful passage in human development. But it is not one that gives Europe much influence elsewhere.

Especially not in Asia. As the Asian economy continues to grow—and Asian political power with it—so it becomes clear that it is Europe whose relative standing will suffer, not that of the U.S. Some European economies are threatened by the growth of low-cost, high-quality manufacturing in Asia. Politically, Europe is a minnow in Asia (arguably, it has been since the old colonial powers were thrashed everywhere from Singapore to Dien Bien Phu) but the U.S. is not. In a region where rivalries of the old sort—between India and Pakistan, say, or China and Japan—might yet kindle into flame, the U.S. acts as a vital balance. The U.S. has been a force in the Pacific for more than 100 years; its role there will be one of the factors—along with the relative youth of its population, its overwhelming military strength and its 200-year tradition of enterprise—that will continue to bolster Washington's strategic significance in the new century.

Beyond the Reach of the State

THE COLD WAR WAS MANY THINGS—AN ideological contest, a military and political one—but it was identifiably a war between states and their allies. Since its end, however, three factors outside the direct control of states have shaped the international system.

The first of these is globalization, the term commonly given to the growing integration of national economies and businesses. Globalization has been at the heart of the most profound development in the world since 1989: the

gloriously saw its divisions wither, also marked the end of its centrality in international affairs. For 200 years, European ideas, European wars, European ideologies and technologies that had their roots in European science together shaped the modern world. That lasted right up until 1989. The Cold War, certainly, was not solely fought in Europe; some of its most dangerous incidents took place in developing nations like Cuba. But domination of Europe—political and ideological as much as military—was its prize.

Twenty years after its annus mirabilis, Europe matters less than it did. This is not to say that

POLAND'S VOICE *Lech Walesa leads a Solidarity rally at the shipyards in Gdansk*

TRIUMPH *Vaclav Havel with Alexander Dubcek, left, as communist power dissolves in Prague*

continued economic rise of Asia. Globalization has not simply improved the life chances of more people in a shorter period of time than has ever been seen before, nor just turned international businesses into significant players; it has presented the world with new strategic possibilities.

The origins of the Asian miracle lay in outward-oriented policies that encouraged integration of local manufacturing capacity with global supply chains, providing jobs for millions. China, above all, benefited from globalization, in more ways than one. After the Tiananmen disaster in 1989, China's leadership was lost and confused. It was not until Deng Xiaoping took his famous southern tour in 1992 that the policies of reform and opening up, which he had encouraged since 1978, got back on track. That saved Communist Party authority. By providing a safety valve for discontent, China's boom helped sustain internal political stability.

But there was more to the boom than that. By linking the Chinese economy to that of the U.S., globalization contributed to global security too. In classic models of international relations, it is easy to see how China and the U.S. might be rivals—one established power, one rising one, both with high degrees of national cohesion and purpose. But with every passing week, as another meeting between American and Chinese officials takes place, as more Chinese students study in the U.S. and more American businessmen travel to meet their suppliers in the Pearl River Delta, so the network of contacts between China and the U.S. grows in strength. These two societies—one the colossus of the 20th century, one that looks optimistically at what the 21st may bring—are coming to know each other well, and knowledge is the essential foundation for mutual trust and respect.

The second factor outside state control that has shaped the world since 1989 is the rise of religious extremism. This did not come out of the blue; Khomeini had taken power in Iran in 1979, and it was already more than 20 years since the Six-Day War had fueled a revival of political Judaism and led Arabs, dismayed by the failure

of secular nationalism, to turn to Islam for succor. Still, most observers missed the significance of radical Islam in 1989. That was an avoidable mistake. Bedraggled Soviet troops had finally left Afghanistan in February, defeated not just by guns and Stinger missiles, but by a conviction on the part of those fighting them that they were engaged in a holy war against an infidel invader. With the benefit of hindsight, it was worth asking: What will those fighters do now? The answer would come soon enough, as radical Islam spilled out of its heartland and took the shape of international terrorism. The long and unfinished fight against terror since 2001 is abundant proof of how hard state powers have found it to confront those who are motivated by millennial religiosity, fighting asymmetric wars.

Third, technology has changed the world. By 1989, personal computers were already commonplace in the West, while cell phones, though they were as big and heavy as a brick, were becoming a status symbol. But in March, unnoticed by all but a handful of enthusiasts, Tim Berners-Lee, a British computer scientist working at the CERN laboratory in Geneva, sketched out the building blocks that enabled the Internet to become a ubiquitous tool of communication and information.

Increased computing power and the Internet have been the essential underpinning of globalization; without them, the unheralded logistics firms in Hong Kong who manage global supply chains would not be able to do their job. And technology has shaken the power of the state in ways that traditional theories of international relations cannot comprehend. In 2009, China's online community rallied to defend a woman charged with killing a man she said was trying to rape her, and protesters on the streets of Iran used Twitter to get their message to the outside world. The disruptive, revolutionary power of technology in even the most autocratic societies has rarely been so evident. It will continue to grow.

We did not quite see that in 1989. But that's forgivable. As a news editor could have told you, in that extraordinary year there was a lot going on. ■

For 200 years, European ideas, wars and technologies together shaped the modern world. That lasted right up until 1989

POUNDING
G.D.R. police spray West Germans as they break through the Wall two days after it first opened

It Happened One Night

The wall that had trapped a people and divided a continent was supposed to stand for 100 years. And then it crumbled

By Anne McElvoy

WHEN DID THE BERLIN Wall cease to exist? I had a ringside seat at the event that would reshape Europe and reverberate across the globe; and still, I couldn't say exactly when that concrete monument to division and folly finally crumbled into dust and souvenirs. No plan existed for the Wall's demise. A country that had a five-year plan for everything from the production of cotton reels to spies and gymnasts could not predict or manage the event that sealed its end.

The German Democratic Republic had fascinated me since childhood, so I'd grabbed every opportunity to travel there throughout the 1980s—the terminal phase of the G.D.R.'s existence, as it turned out. But when I returned in May 1989, the mood had changed. Something bitter and edgy had entered the soul of the semi-nation of 16.7 million Germans. My oldest friend, son of a senior *nomenklatura* professor, hugged me as we stood beside Checkpoint Charlie and I headed off, for the umpteenth time, to a break in what he called "my other world." With a new bitterness in his tone, he murmured *"verdammte Mauer"*— that damn wall. Hungary, one of the countries where East Germans could vacation, had opened its border at the beginning of the month, poking the first hole in the barbed-wire frontier across Europe. The Iron Curtain was rusting.

The elections in the G.D.R. that May were intended to rubber-stamp communist rule. They merely confirmed a sullen atmosphere; even the official statistics revealed a decline in votes for the party line, while concealing the true scale of dissent. East Germans set off on holidays from which many did not return. By August, the streams of small pastel Trabant cars phut-phutting their way south to Dresden and into Czechoslovakia and Hungary told the true story. Seeking out breaches in the Hungarian-Austrian border through which to flee, or holing up in West German embassies, they wanted out. We joked that at this rate only the dissidents and the party bosses would be left to fight it out.

Summer was long, hot and tense. The Czechs, with an equally hard-line government to that of

AT THAT TIME

"At midnight, East Germans [were] free to leave at any point along the country's borders, including the crossing points through the Wall in Berlin, without special permission, for a few hours, a day or forever."
—From TIME's Nov. 20, 1989, cover story

'The only choice was to open up the pressure cooker, or watch it explode.'

—*Günter Schabowski, Communist Party first secretary, East Berlin*

the G.D.R., started to return East Germans and refused to let them through the western border. The fear of being "walled in" even further haunted the young. West German embassies were deluged with *Ossis* seeking asylum. At home, opposition groups, previously consigned to churches and kitchen meetings, flourished. I moved into the vast bronze-windowed monstrosity of the Palast Hotel. You couldn't get a fax without it passing through an office where, a waiter told me, copies were made and sent on to the Stasi, the state's intelligence service. In Erfurt, the grand cathedral city in the south, I befriended a group of young intellectuals: bookbinders, musicians and artists. One subsequently sent me a letter begging me to marry him— the quickest way to gain permission to leave was to wed a Westerner. "Not that I want to disturb your life in any way," he wrote, "but I just have to get out of here."

In autumn, Mikhail Gorbachev came with a breath of Moscow fresh air and publicly wagged glasnost at his truculent host, Erich Honecker. The German party leader played deaf and ordered mass arrests of demonstrators in the middle of East Berlin, just to jolly along the visit. Gorbachev looked grim and issued his Cassandra warning: "Those who come too late will be punished by life." (Being Gorby, he took far longer to say it than that; it was his savvy interpreter who made a memorable phrase of the Russian's comments.) The New Forum opposition movement adopted the slogan "No Violence!"—a demand, but with an undertone of real fear. Rumors of body bags and blood banks were spread to intimidate demonstrators. Honecker gave way to Egon Krenz, a man known unaffectionately as Horse Face, who had built his career as the socialist crown prince and, after decades of party obeisance and Politburo maneuvering, would last precisely 44 days in office.

Avalanche politics swept away one dust-encrusted institution after another. The Central Committee resigned. The Politburo followed. "Who is it today?" the copy taker at the *Times* in London would ask when I phoned up to file another dispatch of mayhem. Power was in the streets, with the protesters and emigrants. WE

ANTHONY SUAU

FACE-OFF
Crowds gather on the Wall after the G.D.R. lifts travel restrictions to the West

ARE THE PEOPLE, read the famous banner. And at last, the people were being heard.

In one sense, the events vindicated the fears of the sclerotic regime: "In our hearts," Hans Modrow, the pro-Gorbachev party chief in Dresden would tell me later, "we knew that the fortified border was what kept this country together. We were stuck in a circular logic: no Wall equals no G.D.R. So the fortified border had to stay, or what was the point of us?"

Honecker, in power since 1971, had predicted "the Wall will still be standing in 50 and even 100 years if the conditions which led to its erection remain unaltered." Looking back at the pace of events, it now all seems like an inexorable roll towards a fall. It certainly didn't feel like that at the time: I guess if you'd asked me, I would have said that, whatever the changes, the Wall would be last to go. It imprisoned our imaginations, as well as those behind it.

A Glorious Time

THE FRIEND WHO HAD BID ME FAREWELL at Checkpoint Charlie joined New Forum. His old schoolmate and Friday-night drinking partner was in the army—and of a senior enough rank, he once let slip, to be tasked with overseeing the burial of the SS20 rocket launchers, trained on the West, in the woods outside Berlin. In this small circle of old friends, the big picture could also be intensely personal. "It could be that one day we'll find ourselves facing each other across the lines," said one friend to the army officer, late one evening. "I won't let that happen," he replied. But there was silence afterward.

Yet for all the unease, it was a glorious time to be in the East. Demonstrators in Leipzig held up posters saying SEND THE STASI TO THE FACTORIES. Signs reading CLOSED FOR TECHNICAL REASONS appeared in shops when too many staff had left the country to run the businesses. (One sign near my flat was changed more candidly to read CLOSED FOR HUNGARIAN REASONS.) The evening news, usually a numbing ritual of party-processed statistical information and announcements of ministerial meetings, became unmissable. Spontaneous gatherings in kitchens and courtyards echoed a new mood of openness: politics ruled by day, parties by night. There was only one topic of conversation: "What happens next?"

In this mood of anxious exhilaration, journalists gathered at the International Press Centre, a Stasi-infected building close to the Wall that had become the center of our daily routine. Theoretically, press from the "nonsocialist

GUY LE QUERREC—MAGNUM PHOTOS

ELATION
Celebrating New Year's Eve near the Brandenburg Gate in Berlin weeks after the Wall fell

economic areas" (the West) had minders who were supposed to keep an eye on us. Really though, there was nothing they could do as we raced around interviewing dissidents like Rainer Eppelman, the "turbulent priest" from the Samaritans Church, and Bärbel Bohley, the feisty doyenne of the opposition who had the distinction of being thrown out by the regime and then bringing a legal case to come back. All the minders could insist on was the odd lunch, presumably to keep up a flow of information about our views of the situation. Even the informers had lost the will to spy.

Between 1 million and 1.5 million adult East Germans had applied to leave the country, no longer fearing recrimination. So at the evening press conference of Nov. 9, as Günter Schabowski, the broad-shouldered Berlin party chief, took the chair, the exodus and its impact—especially on the hospitals and emergency services—loomed over all other considerations. Schabowski was one of the few remotely sympathetic characters of the old Politburo. He'd been a journalist on the party mouthpiece *Neues Deutschland* and fancied himself as good at cut and thrust with Western reporters. He also had a touch of the city's famous uppity attitude and its thick accent, which added a certain comedy to the proceedings.

It was a hot room and I was at the back, taking notes when, shortly before 7 p.m., an Italian reporter asked about the new travel law. Schabowski announced that the Politburo would henceforth permit East Germans to leave the G.D.R. on application. Visas would be issued "without delay." Peter Brinkmann, from the anticommunist West German *Bild Zeitung,* asked whether this would apply to West Berlin, and when the new law would come into effect. *"Ab sofort"* (Immediately), said Schabowski, flicking through his notes in search of validation. "It's a matter for the council of ministers," whispered the minister next to him. Too late.

The British correspondent Daniel Johnson was up next and sounded puzzled. "What will happen to the Wall now?" Schabowski looked stricken: "The permeability of the Wall from our side does not yet and exclusively resolve the question of the meaning of the fortified state border of the G.D.R.," he replied. So there we had it—a wall open, but still closed. Lewis Carroll would have been proud.

Delayed Reaction
NO ONE KNEW WHAT TO DO WITH THIS tangled logic, least of all Schabowski, who hurriedly called the meeting to a close. At the end, he promised "fair and free elections." That would have been sensational news the day before, but we weren't even interested in it. Unthinkables were tumbling by the minute. All that needed to

follow were the bricks in that damn wall. An almighty rush to the scant number of telephones followed, so I decided to run to the nearest border-crossing point at Checkpoint Charlie before the *Times'* evening deadline. The only other journalist with the same idea was Brinkmann, who was intent on finding cheering East Germans. People were either too busy trying to digest Schabowski's gnomic utterances, or hadn't yet seen the news.

On the Leipziger Strasse, which amounted to a showy shopping street by East Berlin's standards, two girls with straggly mid-seventies hairstyles were languidly looking in the shoe-store windows. I ran up to them. "The border's open!" I cried. One shrugged. The other returned to looking at imported stilettos. "She's not quite right in the head," was the last I heard as they ambled off. Brinkmann puffed along, his camera at the ready; I heard his mounting desperation as the first *Ossis* at the Wall's opening stubbornly refused to take it in. "For God's sake," he cried, "can't you just cheer or something?"

The guards were, as usual, distant, sitting high up in their bulletproof boxes. I tried again. "The border's open!" No response. "Herr Schabowski just announced it!" "Well it was still closed a minute ago," snapped his colleague, incontrovertibly. They had "no instructions" and no one had seen the television broadcast. Pending further instructions, etc., etc., I should remove myself immediately from the secure zone. So ended my attempt to breach the Berlin Wall. I hung around and watched a younger guard slip away, a radio to his ear. He gave a little impromptu jig and then straightened his jacket and went back into his box. This was Prussia, after all.

Within hours, the mass of people streaming toward the border crossings had reached such proportions that the Wall had to be opened, which it was, before midnight. Some time later, I sought out Schabowski, who lived in a rather natty apartment by the Spree with his Russian wife Irina and a parrot. "Really, it was a slip of the tongue," he confessed. "When I said 'immediately' I meant that people would present themselves with ID at post offices and form a queue. This was the GDR: it was the only way we could envisage doing anything!" Was there no anger from Schabowski's colleagues for his fateful mistake? "Well, a bit," he recalled. "But then, all things considered, you could say we were all in the s___ together. The only choice was to open up the pressure cooker, or watch it explode."

One People

AFTER DARK, GERMANS POURED THROUGH the Wall, the first still in their nightclothes, sleepwalkers into history. Ten thousand of them partied and hammered, or simply looked around dazed at the strange new world without the Thousand-Year Wall. The next night, the bulldozers began to move in, and the opening became official. I watched it happen in the Bornholmer Strasse, a checkpoint in a suburb near my flat. It had the feel of a neighborhood party, with housebound grandmothers shouting down from the tenements, "Bring me a piece of the Wall up, son!" as if calling for an *apfelstrudel,* and separated families meeting again. When the first chunks of the Wall came flying out, one hit my eye and dislodged my contact lens. (That enabled a claim to my managing editor for "Lost contact lens, due to falling Berlin Wall.") Someone brought out glasses and vodka, with chunks of the Wall's concrete instead of ice in the drinks. Twenty years on, I know a night out doesn't get any better than this.

I would go on to cover the more punitive mood toward East Germany's Stasi oppressors; the unending saga of complicity and blame; the arrival of the deutsche mark and the transition from "We are the people" to "We are one people," as unification became inevitable. It was the birth of a different Europe, free of old divisions and shackles, and one still coming to terms with its variety and responsibility even now. That's the big picture we're marking 20 years on. Yet it's the details that stay freshest in the mind from the autumn that changed the world. One of the great happinesses of my life is that when people ask me, "Where were you in 1989?" I can just say: "I was there." ∎

McElvoy, a former foreign correspondent, is political columnist of the London Evening Standard

> **Ten thousand Germans partied and hammered, or simply looked around dazed**

MAY 25, MOSCOW, U.S.S.R.

AFP/DPA/GETTY

THE KISS *Gorbachev embraces East Germany's hard-line Erich Honecker at 40th-anniversary celebrations for the G.D.R. Weeks later, Honecker—and the Wall—were gone*

Russia's Revolution

Whether he meant to or not, Mikhail Gorbachev gave people the courage to believe freedom was possible

BY PETER GUMBEL

M Y MOST TREASURED SOU-venir of Moscow in 1989 is a white laminated card with a decorative blue border and a sketch of the Kremlin on the front. It's the official menu of the first session of the Congress of People's Deputies, a gathering that started on May 25 of that year and which, in hindsight, marked the beginning of the end of Soviet power.

The menu is very Soviet. The choice of items is limited, the language terse—"bread with cheese," "meat broth"—and the prices ridiculously low. A caviar sandwich cost 56 kopecks, which at the official exchange rate was about 80¢ but in reality about half that or less. The very fact that delicacies such as caviar, iced pastries and oranges were served in the congress canteen at a time of major national food shortages is a reminder of how the Kremlin élite lived in a world of privilege far removed from the everyday hardships suffered by their subjects.

Yet in almost every other way, the proceedings of that congress marked an astonishing break with Soviet tradition. Such gatherings had previously consisted of fawning functionaries voting unanimously in favor of official Communist Party decisions, turning the glass-and-concrete-fronted Palace of Congresses into Rubber-Stamp Central. In 1989, there was none of that. This was the nearest the Soviet system had come to creating a true parliament. The majority of the 2,250 delegates to the congress had been chosen in direct elections that were often contested. They included the famous dissident scientist Andrei Sakharov as well as a clutch of insolent young reformers from the Baltic republics and elsewhere, who would go on to break up the Soviet Union just two years later.

For days, people across the Soviet Union tuned in to live television broadcasts to watch the delegates excoriate the country's leaders for failings that ranged from soap shortages to the all-embracing control of the KGB. There were heckles and insults. The aggressive candor, combined with procedural chaos as party apparatchiks struggled to keep order, made for a gripping spectacle. And there, darting around with a huge grin on his face, was Mikhail Gorbachev, the Soviet leader whose idea it all was.

Nineteen eighty-nine was a colossal year for Gorbachev, who had turned 58 in March. He crisscrossed the globe on a series of historic visits that took him to Havana, London, Bonn, Beijing and Berlin, among other places. Toward the end of the year, after the Berlin Wall had fallen and the communist bloc had begun crumbling from its western flank, he dropped in on Pope John Paul II in Rome and met up with President George H.W. Bush on a storm-tossed boat off the coast of Malta.

I was a foreign correspondent in Moscow at the time, and accompanied Gorbachev on some of his travels. I quickly appreciated that Gorbachev was taking himself, the Soviet Union and the rest of the world on a momentous journey away from rigid doctrine and toward his own increasingly flexible, nondogmatic and—above all—noninterventionist interpretation of reformed socialism. He killed off the Brezhnev

29

Doctrine, which had unblinkingly used military force to defend communism in Eastern Europe, and he did nothing to prevent the demise of old-line party leaders in places like Bulgaria and East Germany, whom he deemed out of touch with reality. In Malta, he and President Bush declared the Cold War over, proclaimed the start of a "new world order" and worked through details of German unification. In his conversation with the Pope, Gorbachev acknowledged the importance of spirituality and freedom of worship.

All the trips were extraordinary in that they unleashed a passion—and sometimes an official fury—in the countries he visited. But over the course of the year, Gorbachev became visibly more confident of his message, even as it ripped through the ideological fabric of the communist world. Gorbachev's domestic critics, and the geriatric leaders throughout Eastern Europe who hated him, complained that all this change would bring down Soviet communism, and of course they were right.

But Gorbachev didn't see it that way. Time and again—before, during and after that revolutionary year—he insisted that he was reforming the system in order to save it. "By the mid-1980s, our society resembled a steam boiler," he wrote in his memoirs, published in 1996. "There was only one alternative—either the Party would lead a process of change that would gradually embrace other strata of society, or it would preserve and protect the former system. In that case, an explosion of colossal force would be inevitable."

Beijing Protests

OF ALL THE TRIPS WE TOOK THAT YEAR, two stand out most vividly: the one to Beijing and Shanghai in May, and the one to East Berlin in October. The trip to China was monumental, marking the official end of three decades of Sino-Soviet suspicion and hostility. Meeting in Beijing's Great Hall of the People on May 16, Gorbachev told the veteran Chinese leader Deng Xiaoping: "Karl Marx lived in the last century and can't provide the answers to all the questions of today." Deng wasn't quite so sure about that, or at least he wasn't about to acknowledge it in public. "Genuine Marxist-Leninists

'All societies have their hotheads who want to renovate society but want to do it overnight.'
—Mikhail Gorbachev

must understand, carry forward and develop Marxism-Leninism," came his reply.

The China trip provided immediate surprises, especially to those of us used to the rationing of basic foodstuffs and daily deprivations of life in Russia. The shops in Beijing and Shanghai overflowed with food and consumer goods. On the streets, it was thrilling to see the energy Gorbachev's presence helped to unleash among students and other protestors—an energy that was tragically crushed in Tiananmen Square a few days after the Soviet leader flew back to Moscow.

The Chinese protests had begun well before Gorbachev arrived, but once he was there, they swelled in number. There were so many people camping out in Tiananmen Square that it was almost impossible to walk across it. In his memoirs, Gorbachev writes about how his hosts were "extremely concerned." He trod carefully. "All societies have their hotheads who want to renovate society but want to do it overnight. But you can't do it overnight," he told Zhao Ziyang, the then General Secretary of the Communist Party.

What a contrast it was back in Moscow for the Congress of People's Deputies. While Beijing had just sent in the tanks, Gorbachev laid on a riotous official celebration of Soviet hotheadedness—and broadcast it live on national TV. Indeed, one of the few sober notes at the congress was its reaction to Tiananmen: a mildly worded statement that urged the Chinese people "to turn this tragic page of their history as soon as possible."

Berlin Bonfire

THE TRIP TO EAST BERLIN IN EARLY October proved even more momentous. Four months earlier, on a visit to the West German capital of Bonn, Gorbachev had received a rapturous welcome from Chancellor Helmut Kohl. The official reception in East Berlin could hardly have been more different. Neither Erich Honecker, the long-serving Communist Party leader, 77 and in failing health, nor his colleagues in the East German Politburo, hid their dislike of Gorbachev's calls for change. "If my neighbor decides to change his wallpaper," chief ideologist

Running Out Of Time

Clunky Soviet *raketa* military watches became the must-have fashion accessory from Milan to New York, as Gorbymania spread in the West. One minor problem: even when they worked, the watches didn't keep time well.

Kurt Hager had said in 1987, "that doesn't mean I have to do the same."

The occasion for the visit was the 40th anniversary of the German Democratic Republic, complete with stiff military parades and set-piece speeches at the hideous concrete-and-glass Palace of the Republic, which has since thankfully been torn down. Signs of trouble abounded: by the time Gorbachev arrived in Berlin, thousands of East Germans had fled to the West German embassy in Prague, Czechoslovakia, seeking asylum, and it was only a matter of time before Hungary and others opened their borders. In Leipzig and other towns, there was growing public discontent that soon led to mass demonstrations. And churches across Berlin turned themselves into ad hoc meeting places for the disgruntled, who turned out in huge numbers to cheer the visiting Russian leader.

As was his custom on official visits, Gorbachev leaped out of his official black Soviet ZIL limousine at one point to talk to people in the street. We all swarmed to hear what he was saying. His snappy, subversive one-liner quickly did the rounds of Germany, East and West: "Those who come too late will be punished by life."

Later that day, standing on a podium during one of the anniversary parades, Gorbachev was greeted by chants of *"Wir sind das Volk!"* (We are the people!) and "Gorby help us." Just behind him was Mieczyslaw Rakowski, the Polish Prime Minister, who spoke both Russian and German fluently. "Do you understand what they are screaming?" he whispered to Gorbachev. "Yes, I understand it," the Soviet leader replied, according to Rakowski. "This is the end."

The Radical

AND SO IT WAS. GORBACHEV LEFT EAST Berlin with no illusions about Honecker's waning hold on power—and not the slightest intention of helping him. As the street protests swelled, the half-million Soviet troops stationed in East Germany were ordered to keep to their barracks and all military maneuvers were canceled. One of Gorbachev's closest aides, Anatoly Chernyayev, recalled that, "The situation was truly explosive. Gorbachev intuitively felt the inevitability of German unification, and he was no longer bothered by the ideological consequences of the disappearance of an outpost of socialism in the middle of Europe."

PETER TURNLEY—CORBIS

The rest is history. These days, many people are credited with bringing down the Berlin Wall, from Ronald Reagan to Pope John Paul II, Lech Walesa and Vaclav Havel. All played a role, as did millions of ordinary men and women throughout Eastern Europe who were sick of the all-intrusive yet dysfunctional system under which they lived. But when I think back to those days in Moscow, or thumb my menu from the Congress of People's Deputies, it's impossible not to marvel at Gorbachev and his Shakespearean role in the drama of that year.

He didn't set out to destroy the entire socialist edifice; in fact, he was keen to rebuild it. But once it started crumbling, he wasn't about to go back on everything he had propagated in a hopeless effort to hold it together. He didn't bring down the Berlin Wall, but having undermined its foundation, he didn't stop it from being toppled, either.

For his role, he is hailed in the West and reviled or ignored at home; today's Russian leaders blame him for allowing the Soviet empire to collapse. "Some say that Gorbachev did not defend socialism, that he more or less 'betrayed his friends,'" he writes in his memoirs. "I firmly reject these accusations. They derive from outdated notions about the nature of relations between our countries. We had no right to interfere in the affairs of our 'satellites,' to defend and preserve some and punish and 'excommunicate' others without reckoning with the people's will … Those who still blame Gorbachev are, in effect, lacking in respect for their own people, who have gained freedom and made use of it as best they could."

Caviar sandwich, anyone? ■

BEAR AND TIGER *Gorbachev and Deng at a May dinner in China. Soon after, Deng sent troops into Tiananmen Square*

ON THE MOVE *Reporters in tow, the President jets to the G-7 economic summit in Paris after stops in Poland and Hungary*

Travels With George

The 41st President's first year in office began quietly and ended in a whirlwind of diplomacy. How the "do-nothing détente" became a voyage to the end of the Cold War

BY MICHAEL DUFFY

MY GOAL, AT THE START OF 1989, was simply not to win the Poppy.

That was the award, created by David Lauter of the *Los Angeles Times,* that would be given to the reporter who had traveled the most miles with President George H.W. Bush in 1989 while publishing ... the least amount of words.

Most of us who covered Bush that year figured we were doomed to win the Poppy. There we were, jetting at 35,000 feet on a chartered Pan Am Clipper to Spokane or Sacramento or Sauk City with all the Veuve Clicquot and Château Margaux we could drink for breakfast, lunch and dinner, but with absolutely nothing to file once we landed. In his early days in office, the 41st President was a tornado of motion—taking in baseball games, golf outings, Chinese restaurants, meetings with just about any group that invited him. He had parties for lawmakers on the South Portico and horseshoe games for aides on the South Lawn. He went everywhere in those first few months, reliably telling audiences, "I really love my job."

But news? Alas, there wasn't much of that. Most of us shadowing Bush feared that we had all lost a sucker's bet: we finally managed to win a coveted reporting spot at the White House only

BETTMANN/CORBIS

THE WORLD STAGE *Only a month into his presidency, Bush visits Beijing, Tokyo and Seoul*

to discover that the man who lived there was determined to keep a low profile. Big presidential moments? Forget it: Bush ordered his motorcades to stop at traffic lights. Momentous Oval Office speeches? No way: his own pollster urged Bush to stay off of television because voters get sick of seeing a President night after night on the evening news. It was just our bad luck to happen along just when America elected someone who desired nothing more than to manage his inbox quietly and let things "prudently" unfold.

Hence the Poppy. And as much as we tried to avoid it, we were all contenders for the prize.

Asking for More Bite

THEN CAME THE SPRING. WE KNEW WELL before inauguration that Bush came into office highly suspicious of Mikhail Gorbachev and the reforms he was putting into place in the Soviet Union. His suspicion wasn't personal, just honed by history. Bush remembered that other Presidents had gotten burned by encouraging dissidents in Hungary in 1956 and Czechoslovakia in 1968, and didn't want a repeat on his watch. He also feared that the Soviet military could not allow Gorbachev to carry on as a reformer forever (a worry that, it's worth noting, would come true in 1991).

Yet if Bush was slow to see Gorbachev had legs, he wasn't entirely deaf to the possibilities either. Early in February, he secretly asked his advisers to come up with a new approach to the Soviets. When their efforts left him underwhelmed, he pushed his team to be more creative, to give him "more bite." We could see something

was up: starting in February, Bush dragged his top advisers (with us in tow) regularly to Kennebunkport, Maine, where he and Secretary of State James Baker, National Security Adviser Brent Scowcroft and deputy National Security Council (NSC) chief Robert Gates, as well as Pentagon boss Dick Cheney and a young NSC Russia expert named Condoleezza Rice, debated how to respond to Gorbachev's steady drumbeat of dramatic arms-control proposals. (The first trip was cramped and cold: Bush and his team met in the master bedroom because it was the only heated room in the house.) This core group differed about whether Gorby was the real thing—and so did his allies. The Germans were pushing Bush to get in the game; Britain's Margaret Thatcher was dragging her feet. Nudged chiefly by Scowcroft and Baker (with Cheney and Gates making skeptical sounds along the way), Bush decided to go for it: he would call Gorbachev's bluff to cut conventional forces in Europe—and then raise it. Most reporters in town had no clue; we were too busy buying mittens at L.L. Bean down the road.

But even though he was moving behind the scenes to catch up, Bush's public management of Gorbachev was ham-handed. His aides blithely dismissed Moscow's many arms-control proposals; his spokesman called Gorbachev a drugstore cowboy. For much of this period Bush endured withering criticism in the press and in foreign policy circles for timidity, for moving too slowly, for being a stodgy cold warrior in the face of obvious, generational change. "Do-Nothing Détente," hissed TIME in an early May headline.

So Bush launched a second wave of travel and a series of speeches to flesh out his plan. We flew to the heavily Polish-American Detroit suburb of Hamtramck to promise aid to the Poles, then to College Station Texas, where, drawing on language drafted by Rice, Bush proposed that NATO move "beyond containment" and, as he put it, "welcome the Soviet Union back into the world order." Bush was trying to get ahead of the curve, but his lofty goals lacked much detail. All these speeches were met with general ho-hums from the foreign policy establishment.

Then, in late May, during a four-nation swing through Europe, Bush unveiled the bold plan he had been hatching for months: deep cuts in troops and matériel in Europe that surpassed Gorbachev's own, both in depth and in the speed with which they could be accomplished, and new talks to reduce short-range nuclear weapons in Europe—the very weapons that had once threatened to tear the alliance apart. After months of taking Gorbachev's proposals only half-seriously, Bush was now offering changes greater than even those the Russian was proposing.

By midsummer, the preferred metaphor around the White House was bait-fishing: easing half a continent out of 50 years of repression, Bush aides said, was like trying to land a 10-lb. fish on a 5-lb. line. It had to be done very carefully. And Bush knew that success might depend as much on manners as on managing the men under arms. On the eve of his July trip to Poland and Paris, he wrote Gorbachev a note reassuring him that he didn't want to stir up any trouble. That surely made it easier for him to meet with Solidarity leader Lech Walesa and shipyard workers in Gdansk. Yet the same instinct proved deeply unpopular when it was revealed that Bush had secretly sent Scowcroft to meet with Chinese leaders in Beijing in the aftermath of the Tiananmen massacre. Those of us on his tail knew that a good story was taking shape: Bush was becoming a man of action—and it was clear he had a penchant for secrecy.

Bush decided to go for it: he would call Gorbachev's bluff to cut forces— and then raise it

As borders and barriers in Europe collapsed in the late summer and fall, Bush warned his aides not to gloat. When the Wall finally fell on Nov. 9, White House aides ushered reporters into the Oval Office, where Bush and Baker had been monitoring events. The President's reaction was muted— and widely mistaken for disappointment. In fact, he was playing down the victory in the Cold War to avoid giving hard-liners in Moscow second thoughts. Critics said Bush was so subdued that it appeared the Berlin Wall had collapsed on him. "I'm very pleased," Bush said, adding that he would not, however, "beat my chest and dance on the Wall." Here, Bush was being prescient as well as prudent: the next day, Gorbachev sent Bush a secret note urging him not to overreact.

And by now, Bush needed and wanted a meeting with Gorbachev; he had been thinking hard about it since July and recorded in his diary that he felt it might be dangerous not to have one. So he proposed the two men meet on ships off the Mediterranean island of Malta. (Why Malta?

Bush's brother had been there and liked it.) There would be no agenda, Bush told reporters— even as he dashed off secret notes to Gorbachev with a list of items for discussion.

If the meeting lacked drama for starters, Neptune kicked it up a notch: the two men arrived in Malta just as a Mediterranean cyclone was making landfall. The first meeting went well: Bush made proposals on everything from economic aid to arms control, including the total elimination of chemical weapons, and the two men talked for four hours; Gorbachev could finally see for himself that Bush was serious about helping *perestroika* succeed. "People criticize me for being cautious and timid. I am cautious," Bush told Gorbachev, "but not timid."

Plans for a second meeting that evening were scuttled by 15-ft. seas—and both men had trouble returning by launch to their respective ships. Soon, Bush was stranded on his cruiser in the Maltese Bay of Marsaxlokk while Gorbachev wisely stayed on the shore, the two leaders barely 2,000 yards apart and unable to speak. Scowcroft prayed that no crisis would erupt elsewhere in the world because the radio gear on the cruiser *Belknap,* where Bush was spending the night, was so antiquated. Most of Bush's staff spent the evening turning green; Bush, the old Navy man, actually went fishing off the bobbing fantail of the *Belknap.* Reporters sheltering on the shore in a leaking medieval fortress were repeatedly driven indoors by the sideways rain. The few U.S. officials on land scrambled to leak everything Bush had proposed before the Soviets beat them to the punch. It was a very long night.

The next day, the weather lifted and the two men held the first ever joint press conference by American and Soviet leaders. It was an almost inconceivable event—and both men could barely suppress grins of elation as the questions and answers unfolded. TIME's cover, out the next evening, pictured Gorbachev and Bush together with the cover line: "Building a New World."

It had been quite a year. And by Christmas, the plans for awarding the Poppy had been set aside. We had all been too busy covering the news to even think about it. ∎

Reagan's Message

The President famously urged Moscow to "tear down this wall." But his speech was more invitation than challenge

BY ROMESH RATNESAR

EIN BERLINER
*The Bran-
denburg Gate
speech, 1987*

DIETER KLAR—DPA/CORBIS

A FEW DAYS AFTER THE FALL OF the Berlin Wall, the journalist Lou Cannon met Ronald Reagan at the former President's office in Century City, Calif. Cannon had covered the White House for the Washington *Post* and had come to interview Reagan for a book on his presidency, *The Role of a Lifetime.* Their conversation turned to Berlin. "Did you ever expect this to happen?" Cannon asked. Reagan shrugged. "Someday," he said.

The legacies of most Presidents are defined by the historical events that transpire on their watch: Lincoln and the Battle of Gettysburg, John F. Kennedy and the Cuban missile crisis, George W. Bush and Sept. 11. But the accomplishment for which Reagan is most widely credited actually took place nine months after he left office. That Reagan has become so linked to the fall of the Berlin Wall—a statue of Reagan unveiled in June 2009 in the rotunda of the U.S. Capitol even has chunks of the Wall embedded in its pedestal—is due largely to an event that took place nearly 18 months before the Wall came down: Reagan's June 12, 1987, address at the Brandenburg Gate, in which he made his famous challenge to Mikhail Gorbachev. The "Tear Down This Wall" speech is often cited by those who claim that Reagan "won" the Cold War. But the speech's true meaning and legacy are far removed from what many Reagan loyalists would have you believe.

Though Reagan's speech at the Brandenburg Gate is the best remembered of his presidency, it was not considered major news at the time. Neither the Washington *Post* nor the New York *Times* ran stories about it on their front pages the next day. Reagan's official biographer, who was in Berlin, called it "an opportunity missed." Frank Carlucci, the President's National Security Adviser, recalls watching Reagan and thinking, "It's a great speech line. But it will never happen." Interviewed by *ABC News,* Henry Kissinger said the speech might prompt the Soviets to relax restrictions in East Berlin somewhat. "But they won't tear down the Wall."

For the next year and a half, the speech remained obscure. The vast majority of Americans would likely have been unable even to identify the phrase *tear down this wall.* But once the Wall came down, it was given new life. All three major U.S. networks played clips of the speech during their nightly newscasts on Nov. 9. President George H.W. Bush cited it during his own speech to the nation from the Oval Office. Interviewed on Nov. 9, Reagan recalled looking across the Wall and seeing East German police preventing people from "getting anywhere near the Wall" to hear his speech. For U.S. conservatives, Reagan's challenge acquired an iconic weight. It defined their image of Reagan. It entered American lore.

And yet it also remains misunderstood. There is little evidence that Reagan's call for the Wall to be torn down had a direct impact on East Germans, or that it inspired them to rise up against their communist rulers. The true significance of Reagan's speech—and its ultimate role in the end of the Cold War—can be found less in the words themselves than in the person to whom they were addressed. Though many of his advisers argued that the central challenge be removed in order not to embarrass Gorbachev, Reagan insisted it stay in for a simple reason: calling on Gorbachev to tear down the Wall might actually inspire him to do it.

Read in that light, the speech is as much an invitation as a challenge. "If he took down that Wall, he'd win the Nobel Prize," Reagan told an aide after the speech. Reagan loathed the Soviet Union and its ideology. But his speech presciently established Berlin as a test of Gorbachev's intentions: if the Soviets truly sought peace and liberalization, Reagan said, they should let the Wall come down. This may be Reagan's greatest legacy: when so many leaders try to intimidate their adversaries by making threats, Reagan defeated his by earning its trust. ∎

Ratnesar's new book is Tear Down This Wall: A City, A President and the Speech That Ended the Cold War

Stonewalling

Reagan first called for the dismantling of the Berlin Wall in a debate televised on CBS in 1967, when he told Senator Robert Kennedy that the "Berlin Wall should disappear."

PATRICK ZACHMANN—MAGNUM PHOTOS

A Chinese Reality

The authorities claimed that they were putting down a
rebellion in Tiananmen Square. That was not the case

BY ADI IGNATIUS

I T WAS CLEAR BY THE START OF THE year that 1989 would be an extraordinary time for China. A free-speech movement had begun to flower at Peking University, where students and some professors held a series of "democratic salons" on the campus lawn. People would stand in a circle and vigorously debate issues that were normally off-limits, like the need for political freedom.

As the *Wall Street Journal's* Beijing bureau chief, I witnessed several of these gatherings. I'd stand at the perimeter listening to the speakers, marveling at their courage. I'd scan the crowd for plainclothes police and usually spot a couple of likely subjects. Yet the participants never seemed cowed. It was all about openness: Why should anyone object to discussions about issues critical to China's future? The leaders were a 19-year-old history major named Wang Dan and the dissident astrophysicist Fang Lizhi. When the dust would settle some months later after Tiananmen, both had been branded public enemies.

But in early 1989 anything seemed possible, and the risk-taking ethos spread far and wide. One of my most vivid memories was the exhilarating avant-garde exhibition at the National Art Gallery in Beijing. For a few days, the walls of the gallery were filled with the whimsical and grotesque variations on Maoist propaganda that would, years later, make some Chinese artists very rich. Banners unfurled on the street outside proclaimed "No U-Turn," hinting that China would never be the same. The dramatic highlight was an installation called *Dialogue,* involving a telephone booth with mirrors inside. Its co-creator, a young woman named Xiao Lu, pulled out a handgun and shot two bullets at the work. The police arrived and shut down the exhibition for the rest of that first day. But a powerful statement had been made. A defiant spirit had been unleashed in China that would eventually lead toward a violent denouement.

All of us seemed like kids at the time—the artists, the activists, the demonstrators, the

SQUARING OFF *A mass rally in the run-up to June 4 during which protesters denounce Deng Xiaoping*

A MOVEMENT
BUILDS
*Truckloads
of supporters
arrive in
Beijing*

PATRICK ZACHMANN—MAGNUM PHOTOS

AT THAT TIME

**"The countdown
began after
Li [Peng]
announced
that 'we must
end the turmoil
swiftly' and
ordered troops
into the city.
While Li's raspy
voice echoed
from Tiananmen
Square's
loudspeakers,
sirens wailed
and blue lights
flashed as an
ambulance
arrived to take
away yet another
weakened
hunger striker …
All waited for
what the new
day would bring."
—From TIME's
May 29, 1989,
cover story**

journalists taking notes—brimming with ambition and churning with idealism and hope. It wasn't always easy for Chinese to mingle with foreign journalists, but we found ways. I used to sneak friends past the official checkpoints into the foreign compound that housed my home and my office. At the end of 1988 my wife—Dinda Elliott, *Newsweek's* bureau chief—and I hosted a Christmas party at our home. The crowd included liberal writers, radical artists, dissidents. I still remember Fang, in his broken English, boisterously singing along to "We Wish You a Merry Christmas."

Danger and Possibility

FOR ME, IT WAS ALL PART OF A LIFE-CHANGING personal journey. I had studied Chinese in college, and so the Beijing posting—and this incredible, unfolding story of a great nation in great flux—marked the culmination of years of focus and passion. Dinda and I were also awaiting the birth of our first child, whose due date was June 4.

The Tiananmen protests themselves began in mid-April. Students at the élite universities, including Wang, assembled initially to mourn the death of Hu Yaobang, who had been purged as head of the Communist Party two years earlier. Hu hadn't been an especially charismatic

figure, and ultimate authority rested with Deng Xiaoping, then 85, who had risen to power after the chaos that followed Mao Zedong's death in 1976. But Hu did at least seem to rule from the heart—a trait other Party officials rarely revealed. He had lost his job in part for refusing to crack down on the liberal trends that were advancing. To many students, he represented the possibility that China could become a normal country after the vindictive power struggles and purges that had long been the norm.

After gathering on campuses to read eulogies and hang commemorative posters, a few students decided to march to Tiananmen Square to unfurl banners honoring Hu. I and a few other foreign journalists learned of this initial march and drove to Tiananmen Square to see what was happening. As with everything I witnessed that year, there was a sense at once of both danger and possibility. Our presence that night was later singled out in a confidential official account as "evidence" that foreign elements were manipulating the movement to damage China and the Communist Party's rule.

In the coming days, Tiananmen Square filled with protesters. They were orderly, peaceful, impassioned, convinced that they needed to speak up for the nation. CNN had set up its facilities to

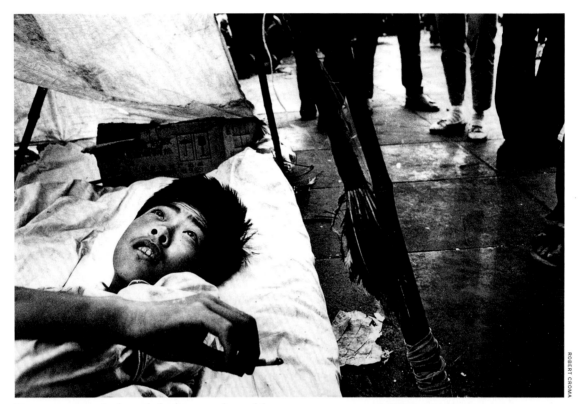

UNCERTAIN DAYS *In the weeks leading up to the crackdown, protesters camp out in Tiananmen Square*

PAUSE BEFORE THE STORM *Young PLA soldiers in Beijing taking a break*

CHAOTIC
STREETS
*Bicyclists
transport a
woman injured
in the violence*

DARIO MITIDIERI—REPORTAGE/GETTY IMAGES

broadcast from the square, and the world tuned in nightly to this intoxicating drama. I remember a white-collar worker who approached me, thrilled to meet a foreign journalist. "Tell the world that the Chinese people want democracy," he said. Like millions of others around the country, he had been moved by the student movement and had joined the marches. My wife, too, experienced the remarkable spirit of that moment. In the first large protests, when students feared they might be stopped with violence, she was in the thick of things. As students pushed through the police cordons, groups of Chinese would lock arms around her to make sure she and our unborn child got through safely. Grannies threw plastic sacks of milk to her from the sidelines. "Please tell our story!" they would shout.

In early May, Dinda flew to Hong Kong to prepare to have the baby. I stayed in Beijing reporting day and night on the protests. On May 23, while I was working late in the office, she called to say she had gone into labor. I flew into action. Yes, I was covering the story of a lifetime. But I was also about to become a father for the first time.

I rushed to Beijing's airport and ditched my car in the parking lot. The airport was jammed with foreigners trying to get out of town. Despite my desperate pleas, no one would give me their ticket. I finally begged a sales agent and got on the next flight to Hong Kong. It made an unannounced stop in Tianjin; a stewardess explained that this was so the pilots could have breakfast. I was dying. This was before the era of cell phones, so I had no way to reach my wife. Finally we

landed in Hong Kong. I cut in front of everyone at customs, immigration and taxi lines and told my cab driver to take me to Matilda Hospital on the Peak. He started driving but then stopped, saying he didn't know the way. I was dumped in a crowded commercial district in Kowloon and had to flag another cab. This one took me to the Matilda. As we drove up the front drive, a nurse emerged. "You must be Mr. Ignatius. Come with me." We ran upstairs to the delivery room. The doctor had given up on me and was finally telling my wife it was time. "Push," he instructed, just as I entered the room. Within minutes, Oliver was born.

Pawns in a Power Struggle

TWELVE DAYS LATER, ON JUNE 4, THE Tiananmen massacre took place. I was still in Hong Kong. While I regret not being in Beijing to bear witness to the tragedy, my absence in a sense helps expose as untrue China's official explanation for its violent response. For by early June the movement was starting to flag. Many foreign journalists decided then to finally take long-overdue R&R breaks after weeks of intense coverage. The Beijing-based students had largely returned to their campuses. And while a flow of students was still arriving from outside the capital, the protests were losing their momentum.

The fact is, the students had become pawns in a power struggle at the pinnacle of the Party. The hard-line faction within China's leadership had taken control and had the army at the ready. On May 19, these men had voted to declare martial law. Zhao Ziyang, an economic reformer who had

43

PETER TURNLEY—CORBIS

UNHEEDED
A protester pleads with a military officer to halt the crackdown on the square

replaced Hu as Party leader in 1987, had refused to sign off on the plan and was ousted. The only question was when and how the assault would take place. I suspect the hard-liners wanted to crack down so defiantly that they would wipe away not only the protesters but also the liberal political ideas that were beginning to take root.

The Party's official line is that it put down a rebellion, just as any right-minded government would do. The reality was different. The protesters still on the square were orderly and, as their numbers dwindled, on the verge of becoming irrelevant. But on June 2, the Party without warning sent thousands of troops rushing in toward the center of the city. Unarmed, they accomplished only one thing: ensuring that much of Beijing took to the streets again in agitated concern.

And the next night the soldiers returned, this time in tanks or armed with machine guns. Eyewitnesses reported indiscriminate shooting into the crowds. If China's leaders faced, as they later claimed, a violent rebellion, it was because they had created one. By the early hours of June 4, hundreds of citizens were dead. Wang Dan, the

young man who had led those democracy salons, topped the most-wanted list of fugitives after the massacre and was arrested within a month. (Years later, he was allowed to leave for the U.S.) Fang Lizhi took refuge in the U.S. embassy, where he would remain for a year before China let him emigrate.

Immediately after the violence, I returned to Beijing. My wife and son joined me a few weeks later. It was a grim scene. The sense of hope had been crushed. Few would even dare talk to a Western journalist. Most of our Chinese friends laid low; it was months in some cases before we even knew whether they had survived the massacre. Official goons in cars and on motorcycles followed us whenever we went out. Knowing our phones were tapped, we made up false rendezvous, hoping security agents would take the bait and waste their time staking out our false leads.

The country fell into a deep darkness that would start to turn only in 1992, after we had left Beijing, when Deng Xiaoping realized the country had veered off in the wrong direction. He took a celebrated trip to the freewheeling south and

called for a reinvigoration of China's capitalist-style reforms, restarting many of the initiatives that his onetime protégé, Zhao, had championed. The Chinese economic juggernaut was under way. But political freedom has yet to flower.

Power Book

AS FOR ZHAO, HE WOULD SPEND THE LAST 16 years of his life under house arrest, out of the public eye. He died in 2005. It had been assumed, and lamented, that he never left a memoir about the events of 1989. Was he too bitter? Too feeble? Too tightly controlled? In fact, under the nose of his captors, he was secretly recording his take on what really happened during Tiananmen.

More than a year before Tiananmen's 20th anniversary, I was brought in on that secret by Bao Pu, the political activist whose father, Bao Tong, had been Zhao's closest aide. The younger Bao had been tasked with assembling and translating, in Hong Kong, the 30 hours of tapes Zhao had secretly recorded. Bao Pu brought me in as a co-editor, and in May 2009 Simon & Schuster released *Prisoner of the State: The Secret Journal of Premier Zhao Ziyang.* The book can't be sold in mainland China. But unauthorized versions of the Chinese-language edition are being downloaded across the country. Zhao's memoir will reveal to many Chinese the extent of the disagreement at the highest levels on how to respond to the Tiananmen protests. They will learn that some top officials advocated a softer approach and a tolerance for dissent that they argued didn't threaten the Party or the nation. The killings, in other words, didn't have to happen.

Yet the victims of Tiananmen did not die in vain. The crackdown produced deep anguish around the world. Later in that tumultuous year, when the winds of protest arrived in East Germany, leaders there faced a similar choice. In the end they avoided bloodshed. They opened checkpoints at the Berlin Wall, and the East bloc was on its way toward gaining its freedom.

Someday, the Chinese will have their day too. ∎

Ignatius is editor in chief of the Harvard Business Review

THE DAY AFTER *Residents pass charred PLA vehicles, torched by angry civilians*

45

Tibet's Nobel Man

The Dalai Lama's Nobel Peace Prize was not the culmination of Tibet's struggle—but simply one stage

BY PICO IYER

MICHAEL O'NEILL—CORBIS OUTLINE

THE DALAI LAMA CAME OUT OF his room with hands extended, as open and relaxed as if it were just another day. Twenty-four hours earlier, he had been awarded the Nobel Prize for Peace, while enjoying a meeting outside Los Angeles with scientists. I was intruding on him with questions for TIME and entered a modest ranch house where busy aides were dealing with congratulatory phone calls and faxes from around the globe. It was a moment of great hope and possibility for Tibet and its supporters, but the Dalai Lama was characteristically measured, as if this were just another step on a long path with no short-term guarantees.

The minute he saw me, in the bright October sunshine, he grabbed me by the hand—as he would have grabbed anyone—and whisked me off into a small room where we could talk. Our first few minutes in the room, he looked around for a chair in which I (not the new Nobel laureate) would be comfortable. Then he looked at me directly, and said, "How should I spend the money?" At the moment when less realistic friends were claiming that Tibet's struggle was won, he said, "I really wonder if my efforts are enough." According to his Buddhist teaching, almost no victory is permanent, nor any loss.

Though Tibet had been occupied by People's Liberation Army troops 30 years before—moving the Dalai Lama to flee into exile—the Tibetan struggle for freedom had suddenly gained momentum in the months leading up to 1989. When monks in Lhasa began crying out for independence in 1987 and were suppressed, often violently, by Chinese soldiers, the Dalai Lama set about outlining a new policy in which he no longer called for independence for Tibet from China, only meaningful autonomy. And even after Beijing responded to his suggestion with more violence—demonstrations in March 1989 left 250 unarmed Tibetans dead in Lhasa and the city under martial law—the Dalai Lama

According to his teaching, almost no victory is permanent, nor any loss

continued to speak calmly for interdependence, dialogue and peace. In rewarding him, the Nobel committee seemed to be sending a larger message to the world that velvet revolutions could achieve more than the Tiananmen protests ever did.

Yet, 20 years on, the Dalai Lama's circumspection on that sunny day looks like prescience, as Tibet is ever more in Beijing's grip, and 20 years closer to losing its distinctive identity. In Burma Aung San Suu Kyi, who was placed under house arrest that July (and rewarded with her own Nobel Prize two years later), is still in confinement, trying to outwit a brutal dictatorship. If 1989 means anything in Asia, it is that no hero of conscience can be sure of quick success.

But what the Tibetan leader—and others—were offering in that year sowed the seeds for a new sense of global responsibility. The first obligation of any Tibetan, the Dalai Lama was stressing with his new policy, was to work with China and look for common ground; in a planetary neighborhood, attacking what you see as your enemy is as senseless as punching yourself. And if China truly saw Tibet as part of itself, then it should try to help Tibet, with much-needed material and modern developments, without feeling the need to oppress it. The Nobel Committee effectively underlined this sense of interdependence by helping turn the Dalai Lama and his people from remote characters in a faraway kingdom to members of the global neighborhood.

By the time the Dalai Lama went to Oslo to accept the award, "on behalf of the Tibetan people," near the end of the year, he had answered the question he posed to me. Some of the prize money went to Mother Teresa for her work with the poor. Some went to Africa, to help the hungry. And some went to Costa Rica, to help fund a university for peace. As 1990 began, it was hard for anyone to deny that the concerns of anywhere, in a global neighborhood, are the concerns of everywhere else. ■

About Turn

When Vietnamese troops left Cambodia in 1989, photographer Philip Blenkinsop went with them. What do the two countries look like today?

BY HANNAH BEECH/PHNOM PENH TO HO CHI MINH CITY

PHOTOGRAPHS BY PHILIP BLENKINSOP—NOOR

W HEN THE FINAL VIET- namese soldiers straggled out of Cambodia in September 1989, after a decade's bloody occupation, the convoys rumbled home in rusting Soviet trucks. Army meals consisted of little more than water drawn from nearby rice paddies and cubes of pork fat. Many of the Cambodians who lined the rutted road to watch the departing soldiers were lucky to eat even that. The only constant in their mouths was the metallic taste of fear. Vietnam was desperately poor, Cambodia even poorer.

Today, the five-hour drive between the booming Cambodian capital Phnom Penh and the even more rollicking Vietnamese metropolis of Ho Chi Minh City rolls by on shining asphalt, as smooth as the relations between once bitter enemies. On the Cambodian side of the border, a cluster of factories called the Manhattan Special Economic Zone and a triumphal stand of casinos—the Caesar, the VIP, the Win—attest to the new money flooding the region. Vietnam and Cambodia are still poor, and income inequality is widening. But their economies expanded at 6.2% and an estimated 6.5% respectively in 2008 and were preceded by years of double-digit growth.

EXODUS *Vietnamese troops share a moment of laughter as they depart Cambodia in Soviet-made trucks and head home*

Foreign countries once sent weapons; now they invest in garment factories and office towers.

In the context of the great upheavals of 1989, the ebb of a distant war between Cambodia and Vietnam might feel like a historical footnote. But this conflict, the only sustained war between communist countries, represented the climax of Cold War geopolitical machinations that directly claimed tens of thousands of lives in Indochina. A decade before, Vietnam, supported by the Soviet Union, invaded its neighbor ostensibly to free the country from the Khmer Rouge, which presided over the deaths of up to one-fifth of the Cambodian population. The Khmer Rouge, backed by Beijing, had invited trouble when they made incursions into southern Vietnam in a deluded effort to seize what centuries ago had been Cambodian territory. After the Vietnamese swept away the Khmer Rouge from Phnom Penh, a puppet regime was installed. But a bloody drip-drip of combat between Vietnamese soldiers and Khmer Rouge guerrillas prevented either country from contemplating a future of peace or prosperity.

A series of meetings in Jakarta and Paris in 1989 cobbled together an unlikely détente

ONE CITY, TWO FACES *Ho Chi Minh City's Cholon Chinatown district in 1989, far left. Luxury brands now preen in the city, left*

between warring Cambodian factions and Hanoi. When the Vietnamese pulled out of Cambodia, it not only signaled the decline of socialist fervor in Southeast Asia; it also unleashed an economic transformation that has uplifted millions. "Only after the withdrawal could we see the light at the end of the tunnel in terms of our economy and foreign relations," says Huynh Buu Son, a Vietnamese former state banker. "This was a turning point for Vietnamese history—and for the region."

For years after the Vietnamese quit Cambodia, the upturned earth near the international airport in Phnom Penh was still known as the Place of Vietnamese Corpses. By the Vietnamese army's own reckoning, its occupation of Cambodia resulted in 25,300 Vietnamese deaths. The soldiers' bodies were eventually repatriated from Phnom Penh, but the vast plot lay unused afterward. It was a place, people whispered, of restless ghosts. Then, as a building boom struck the Cambodian capital, the local Canadia Bank snapped up the Place of Vietnamese Corpses and redeveloped it as a housing estate. Duong Bela, a former conscript in the Cambodian army who served the Vietnamese occupiers, is one of

CULTURE CLASH *Khmer* apsara *dancers bid farewell to Vietnamese troops as they pass Phnom Penh's Royal Palace in 1989, above; a wedding party in Ho Chi Minh City, 2009, right*

FOR TIME

the proud home owners. He's not worried about any ghosts in his new home. "That was a long time ago," he says. "We've all moved on."

So has neighboring Vietnam. Around the time Hanoi was readying to pull out of Cambodia, Son, a native of Saigon—as locals still refer to what was renamed Ho Chi Minh City—was busy resuscitating the Vietnamese economy. After 14 years of socialist experimentation, the country's planned economy had unraveled. Son drafted the country's first banking reform and was feted in Paris and Washington for his economic derring-do. "It was time to change," recalls Son. "Everyone knew it."

The same year, Son and other reformers submitted a plan for socialist Vietnam's first foreign-investment zone. The formation of the Tan Thuan Export Processing Zone was predicated on Vietnam quitting Cambodia, since a withdrawal was a precondition for many countries normalizing economic relations. Today, 30,000 Tan Thuan workers, on the outskirts of Ho Chi Minh City, churn out everything from bridal gowns to circuit boards for export to Germany, Australia, the U.S. and elsewhere.

These days, it is Ho Chi Minh City that has been invaded—by Marc Jacobs and Cartier and Gucci. Their boutiques preen on streets where bedraggled North Vietnamese troops once marched into town. Despite a property downturn, nearly everything in Vietnam's financial capital seems on the brink of demolition for something newer or bigger or taller. Driving the streets, Bui Quang Sac complains that almost nothing is where it used to be—a sense of disorientation is practically the only constant in this changing city. When he was 18, Sac was drafted to fight in Cambodia. On the way to the front lines, he fled. A dozen of his platoon of 40 perished. Sac ended up in a re-education camp for two years for his army desertion. "But at least I lived," he says, weaving through a dense traffic of cars, trucks and a fleet of motorcycles laden with entire families. For those Vietnamese and Cambodians who made it past 1989, just surviving was an accomplishment. Now the real living has begun. ■

HYBRID NATIONS *Vietnamese soldiers and Khmer civilians await a ferry at a Mekong River crossing, 1989, top; Sok Kong, part Vietnamese and one of Cambodia's richest businessmen, enjoys the good life, 2009, above*

Setting a Tone For History

The meeting between F.W. de Klerk and Nelson Mandela made a miracle possible in South Africa

By Alex Perry/Cape Town

SP OBSERVES THAT PROBLEMS ARE there to be solved; life is fraught with problems. M. concurs and comments that however large problems become, there is always hope that they can be solved ... SP says he has emphasized ... the necessity for Africa to come to terms with the Afrikaner ... M. says he fully appreciates this and has come to know the Afrikaner better in prison."

It is July 5, 1989. "SP" is South African President P.W. Botha and "M." is Nelson Mandela. These minutes, taken by Niel Barnard, the then head of South Africa's National Intelligence Service, record how, after 41 years of apartheid and 26 years in jail for Mandela, a white-supremacist President and a black revolutionary leader took the first steps toward peace. Mandela had been snuck through a back door into Botha's official residence in Cape Town, Tuynhuys ("Garden House" in Afrikaans). Botha poured the tea—a gesture of respect unthinkable under the white rule that prevailed. The discussion was short, just half an hour, and skirted the big issues. But after it, as Mandela records in his autobiography, *Long Walk to Freedom,* "there was no turning back."

A little over five months later, Mandela was escorted from jail to Tuynhuys once again to meet Botha's successor, F.W. de Klerk. This time the discussion was more substantial. Mandela demanded de Klerk release him and his comrades, lift the ban on Mandela's party, the African National Congress (ANC), and end the state of emergency. De Klerk made no promises, but did not argue either. "From the first I noticed that Mr. de Klerk listened to what I had to say," wrote Mandela. "Mr. de Klerk ... was a man we could do business with." Crucially, de Klerk's reaction matched Mandela's. "The first time I met Mandela ... I noticed how good a listener he was," de Klerk told me. "I reported back to my constituency and said: 'This is a man I can do business with.'" Less than two months later, de Klerk, whose previous reputation as a hard-liner belied an equally hard-nosed practicality, lifted the ban on the ANC. On Feb. 11 Mandela, by then 71, walked out of prison with a simple message. De Klerk was a "man of integrity," he told a crowd of thousands in Cape Town. A settlement was possible.

What followed would often be less than a fairy tale. During the negotiations to end apartheid, Mandela accused de Klerk of resisting majority rule and "waging a covert war" against the ANC, with the Zulu Inkatha Freedom Party (IFP) as its proxy. "Our relationship was up and down," admits de Klerk today. But the way was set. The Tuynhuys meetings had laid the foundations for a new country. "After that, the end of apartheid became inevitable," says Allister Sparks, whose book *Tomorrow Is Another Country* documented the transition. The path to the first free elections was marred by violence and killings—there were attacks by whites on blacks, by blacks on whites, and thousands died in township battles between the ANC and the IFP. But because the change had begun in cordial discussion, it did not, as many feared, lead to civil war. "Even when it was testy, we always found it possible to raise the issue above the tension so that the process could move forward," says de Klerk. Black did not eject white in a violent overthrow. Whites did not circle the wagons and fight to the last man. Instead, in 1994 South Africa held an election, and Mandela won.

The Tuynhuys effect resonated way beyond South Africa. Africa was reunited with its greatest leader and the world gained a man who quickly became a kind of universal conscience. It also set a global precedent. The end of apartheid was not, as many took it at the time, primarily a story of improving race relations with parallels in American desegregation—though healing the race divide was certainly an objective. Rather, as Sparks says, it was first and foremost about confronting a conundrum all too common around the world: how to bind together two nations in one state. "It's like Israelis and Palestinians," says Sparks. "Or Protestants and Catholics in Northern Ireland." The miracle of South Africa is that the attempt more or less succeeded.

Despite many setbacks and a persistent racial distrust, a new multicolored South Africa—a Rainbow Nation, in Archbishop Desmond Tutu's phrase, where color is no longer a legal distinction, and a diminishing social and cultural one—is an emerging reality. Middle-class black

ILLUSTRATION FOR TIME BY DAVID HUGHES

South Africans now number in their millions. Johannesburg, the business capital, is home to a new black élite. Afrikaners, courted assiduously first by Mandela and now again by new President Jacob Zuma, are finding a place under this new banner. "Afrikaners have been in Africa as long as whites in America," says Sparks. "In giving up their country, the big question was what would still define them as a people?" The answer was culture. Afrikaners discovered their identity did not derive primarily from political power. That is gone today, but Afrikaner arts—from literature and art to cookery and rock festivals—is in renaissance. "And its theme is: we are South Africans," says Sparks.

Questions of identity and nationhood are some of the most fundamental in politics. For South Africa's rulers, old and new, they were defining everything else. As he later admitted, Mandela did not spot the danger of HIV/AIDS until it was well on its way to killing 2.8 million people and infecting 5.7 million in South Africa alone. The ANC saw reports of South Africa's violent crime in racial terms, as a Western attempt to denigrate Africans. Mandela's successor Thabo Mbeki even regarded AIDS as a Western drug-company conspiracy. Under the ANC millions of South Africans have been connected to electricity and water and given real homes. But, shamefully, inequality and the number living in poverty has actually grown. In the end, South Africa's great triumph was also a great distraction. Twenty years later, the Tuynhuys meetings still resonate—not least in the minds of their participants—but millions of South Africans find their more immediate concerns go unnoticed in the shadow of this towering history.

For a country facing such daunting challenges, perhaps the greatest legacy of Tuynhuys is the spirit in which the meetings were convened. As Mandela said: "However large problems become, there is always hope that they can be solved." Botha had poured the tea. And the principle that simple act established—pragmatism for the sake of peace—has endured. On April 14, 1994, four years after they first met and 13 days before South Africa's first free general election, de Klerk and Mandela, by then joint Nobel Peace Prize winners and rival party leaders, held a televised debate. De Klerk criticized the ANC's spending plans. Mandela accused de Klerk of fanning race hatred and opposing redistribution to blacks. "But as the debate was nearing an end, I felt I had been too harsh," Mandela wrote in *Long Walk to Freedom*. "In summation, I said, 'The exchanges between Mr. de Klerk and me should not obscure one important fact. I think we are a shining example to the entire world of people drawn from different racial groups who have a common loyalty, a common love, to their common country ... We are going to face the problem of this country together.' At which point I reached over to take his hand ..." South Africa's miracle, the story of how in two short meetings the most bitter of enemies learned to drop their fists and try a handshake instead, still illuminates the world with hope. ∎

CRIME SCENE *The Peshawar street corner today where Azzam,*
far right, and two of his sons were killed in a 1989 bomb blast

Who Killed Abdullah Azzam?

How the mysterious assassination of an Arab leader of Afghanistan's anti-Soviet jihad changed the face of global terrorism

By **Aryn Baker**/
Peshawar

ON THE MORNING OF NOV. 23, 1989, Waheed Muzhda, an Afghan translator working in Peshawar, Pakistan, for one of the most important Arab leaders of the anti-Soviet jihad, noticed something peculiar on his way to work. Laborers had blocked off a small intersection leading to a mosque popular with the Afghan Arabs, as the foreign jihadis were called, and were cleaning the drainage culvert of accumulated garbage. At work, Muzhda joked with his colleagues that the mayor had probably received funds for a neighborhood cleanup, but would spend only enough to prepare one corner for an official inspection.

The next day, Muzhda's boss, a charismatic Palestinian preacher called Abdullah Azzam, left his house for the Arab mosque where he was due to lead the Friday prayer. A month before, unknown men had planted a bomb under the minbar from which he usually preached. It had been spotted by a cleaner before the service, but Azzam knew there would be other attempts on his life. Still, he shrugged off the threat, telling journalist Jamal Ismail, "My destiny is already written. Nothing I can do will prevent what is meant to happen."

That November morning, Umme Mohammad, Azzam's wife, waved goodbye to her husband and two sons, Mohammad, 23, and Ibrahim, 14, as they drove to the mosque, then turned to the kitchen where she began to prepare the evening meal. A few minutes later she heard a loud explosion. A plume of black smoke filled the sky from the direction of the mosque. "I already knew," she told me recently, sitting in her living room in Amman, Jordan. But she called the office anyway. "I asked, 'Was it the mosque, or the car?' 'The car.' My husband and sons had become martyred."

The explosion was witnessed by Jamal Azzam, Abdullah Azzam's nephew and assistant, who was following Azzam's car as it passed over the culvert where Muzhda had spotted the cleaning crew the day before. "There was a loud noise and the car jumped in the air," says Jamal Azzam. When the smoke cleared he saw that the car had been blown in two. Mohammad's body had been thrown into a tree. Ibrahim's legs were tangled in the electrical wires overhead, while his hands landed across the street. But Azzam's body was hardly scratched, Jamal says. "There was just a little blood coming from his mouth."

The bomb that killed Azzam was not packed with nails or shrapnel, which may have been intentional. If no Pakistanis were killed, the investigation would be cursory at best. "Nobody paid attention to the Arabs," says district leader Mansoor Elahi. "Normally when something like this happens the investigators try to figure out the man's enemies, but because he was a

foreigner, no one took the time to look." If they had, it might not have helped. A lot of people wanted Abdullah Azzam dead.

Revered and Reviled

AT THE TIME, AZZAM'S MURDER BARELY registered outside the Arab world and the rough borderlands that unite and divide Afghanistan and Pakistan. Yet it is easy to argue that his assassination was the critical turning point in the development of al-Qaeda, the extremist network that has defined the global war on terror. Azzam was a man who was widely revered—to

ADAM FERGUSON—VII MENTOR PROGRAM FOR TIME

PAYING RESPECTS *A man prays at Peshawar's Pabi Graveyard of the Shuhadaa (Martyrs) where Azzam is buried*

this day, friends, relatives and students speak of him in glowing terms, calling him "an angel," "a holy man," "generous." If he had lived, says his son, Hutaifa, "there would have been no September 11."

But Azzam was also reviled, and feared, for his power to inspire others to share his dedication to jihad. There were no fewer than five assassination attempts on Azzam in the months leading up to his death, says Hutaifa, and countless threats. In the teeming, faction-ridden streets of Peshawar, they could have been launched by one group or several. "Who didn't want to kill Azzam?" asks journalist Ismail, who worked with Azzam and covered the anti-Soviet resistance throughout the 1980s. He counts the possibilities on his fingers: "There was the KGB and KHAD [the intelligence service of the communist government in Afghanistan] because he was a powerful leader in the jihad. Israel and Mossad, because he helped found Hamas. The [Pakistan] government of Benazir Bhutto, which came to know that he helped instigate a no-confidence vote against her in Parliament." There were the Americans, because Azzam objected to their efforts to reconcile the *mujahedin* with the Afghan government after the Soviets left; Shi'ite elements in Iran who saw him as chief of the Sunnis; Gulbuddin Hekmatyar, a powerful Afghan warlord who resented Azzam's support of a rival; and other Arabs, who were concerned about his growing power. "The only person I can say for a fact didn't kill him is myself, because I was getting married in Jordan that day," says Ismail.

Barrel-chested, with a long black beard streaked with white, by 1989 Azzam had become a familiar figure on the streets of Peshawar and in the battlefields of Afghanistan, where he was

Pen and sword
Al Jihad
magazine,
published by
Azzam and
bin Laden to
glorify their
fight against
those whom
they considered
infidels

known as the godfather of jihad. Born in Jenin in 1941, Azzam fled to Jordan after Israel captured the West Bank in 1967. He studied at Cairo's Al-Azhar University, then taught at King Abdulaziz University in Jeddah, Saudi Arabia, where he met a quiet, pious student, the son of a rich Saudi construction magnate, who became his patron. Until his death and beyond it, Azzam would be linked to that student—Osama bin Laden.

When the Soviets invaded Afghanistan in 1979, Azzam, who felt humiliated by the occupation of his homeland, found an outlet for his rage. In a 1984 book he advanced a new theory, declaring that religious war to liberate Muslim lands from foreign occupation was compulsory for all Muslims—as important as praying, fasting and tithing. The book galvanized an international Islamist movement, and not long after it was published, Azzam himself moved to Peshawar, the staging area for the anti-Soviet resistance, where he set up the Makhtab al-Khadamat, or Services Bureau, to organize the influx of Arab volunteers. Bin Laden, whose wealth provided the Arab jihadis with plane tickets, housing and expenses, backed him. Together they published *Al Jihad* magazine, a full-color monthly that

glorified battle, denounced the atrocities of the Soviets and asked for donations. But after the Soviets withdrew in 1989, funding for the resistance from the U.S. and Saudi Arabia dried up. In Peshawar, a city crawling with opium smugglers, arms merchants and intelligence agents, jihad had become as much a business as a religious calling. Deprived of a cause, the Arab Afghans argued about where the jihad should go next and squabbled over shrinking resources. Bin Laden, with his deep pockets, was the prize.

Azzam argued for taking the jihad back to Palestine. But a newly radicalized group of Arabs led by the Egyptian doctor Ayman al-Zawahiri was gaining strength. Al-Zawahiri was a *takfiri,* one of those Muslims with an extreme belief in the evil of apostasy, and urged the overthrow of Arab regimes such as Egypt's and Saudi Arabia's, which he declared had strayed from the true path. Azzam stuck with the conventional doctrine that Muslims should not kill Muslims. As the embodiment of jihad and bin Laden's mentor, Azzam was hence an obstacle both to al-Zawahiri's ambition to foment Islamic revolution, and to his desire to get bin Laden to fund it.

In the early summer of 1989, as Afghanistan started collapsing into civil war, bin Laden and al-Zawahiri convened a meeting that formalized the establishment of an élite fighting force destined eventually to use terror to achieve its aims. The new recruits, who signed an oath of fealty to bin Laden, eventually became known as al-Qaeda, or "the Base," after the camp where they trained. Azzam was appalled, according to his Algerian confidant and later son-in-law Abdullah Anas: "He was against the method of trying to recruit people not for jihad in Afghanistan but for planning to do something else." Al-Zawahiri retaliated by calling Azzam a CIA spy.

A Multitude of Motives

FOR ALL THAT BITTER HISTORY, ON THE rare occasions that the Afghan Arabs once allied to Azzam meet, few believe that the enmity between him and al-Zawahiri led to the assassination. "Zawahiri was a nobody," scoffs Umme Mohammad. "He didn't have the power or the following to do something like that." Muzhda, Azzam's translator, isn't so sure: "Peshawar was a city where if you had money, you could pay to get any work done, from street-cleaning to assassinations."

That is doubtless true, but there were others besides al-Zawahiri and his supporters who could have availed themselves of the same services, and had every reason to want to. As the Soviets withdrew, the Afghan *mujahedin* factions, deprived of a common enemy, fell upon each other in the beginnings of a brutal civil war that would last five years and eventually usher the Taliban into power. The Afghan Arabs were forced to take sides. Most, including al-Zawahiri, allied with Hekmatyar, a fearsome Pashtun warlord who also benefited from support from Pakistan's intelligence agencies—the very people who would have run any investigation into Azzam's assassination. Azzam backed Hekmatyar's great rival, Ahmad Shah Massoud, an ethnic Tajik whom he anointed "the new hero of jihad"—and who was eventually murdered by an al-Qaeda hit squad two days before the attacks on the World Trade Center and the Pentagon. Azzam's embrace of Massoud infuriated Hekmatyar. "The first thing that came to mind when I heard the news of Azzam's death was that Hekmatyar was behind it," says Abdullah Abdullah, Massoud's aide and later Afghanistan's Foreign Secretary. "There was a lot of money being channeled to Hekmatyar at the time, and Azzam's support for Massoud would have had an impact on that."

Still, argues journalist Ismail, there were other groups who would have had more invested in seeing Azzam dead. Like al-Zawahiri, Azzam saw Afghanistan's potential as an international jihad training ground. Soon after the launch of the Palestinian *intifadeh* in 1987 and the formation of Hamas, an openly Islamist branch of what had up to then been a Palestinian resistance dominated by secular nationalists, Azzam started taking young men from Palestine to Afghanistan to train in special camps. The Palestinians went in under false passports, to protect them from Israeli intelligence. But the existence of the camps came to light after a foiled car bombing at a Marriott hotel in Tel Aviv. The would-be bombers confessed, which led to the discovery of several militant cells throughout Israel, the West Bank and Gaza. "They didn't know anything about each other," says Ismail. "Their only common link was that they had all trained against Israel in Azzam's camps." A blunt warning to Azzam arrived by a curious messenger—a representative of Yasser Arafat's Palestine Liberation Organization, which Azzam had long dismissed for its secular ideology, went to Peshawar. "Israel is after you," the envoy told Azzam, according to Ismail. "Take care." "That was the beginning," says Hutaifa. "Mossad knew that my father had built a very strong foundation against Israel, and that after Afghanistan it would be Israel's turn." Jamal, Azzam's nephew, is convinced Mossad was behind his death.

The Israelis may indeed have had a motive. But nobody has come close to showing that they killed Azzam. Ahmad Zaidan, a Syrian journalist who covered Azzam's assassination, throws up his hands in exasperation when asked who might have planted the bomb. "It's an enigma," he says, "just like the others. Who killed [John F.] Kennedy? Who killed Benazir Bhutto? I can't make up my mind who would have wanted to kill him the most."

> **'Hijacking airplanes, explosions in the public places—that is not what Abdullah Azzam called a jihad.'**
> —*Abdullah Anas, Abdullah Azzam's son-in-law*

Would history have been different if Azzam had lived? He was no angel, by any standards other than those of jihadis. But many believe that he would have been a moderating force on bin Laden, and that his scholarship and charisma would have tempered al-Zawahiri's crazy radicalism. Azzam's son-in-law, Anas, thinks that Azzam would have continued his mission to liberate Muslim lands from the grip of infidels. "He called people to fight in Afghanistan because it was occupied by the Soviets," Anas says. "If he saw what happened in Iraq and what is happening in Palestine he would say the same thing. But what is going on in the name of jihad, killing civilians, kidnapping, hijacking airplanes, explosions in the public places—that is not what Abdullah Azzam called a jihad."

It is a comforting thought, up to a point, but we will never know if it is well founded. Nor, probably, will we ever know who blew up a car in Peshawar in 1989. A lot of people wanted Abdullah Azzam dead. —WITH REPORTING BY WILLIAM LEE ADAMS/LONDON AND ERSHAD MAHMUD/PESHAWAR ∎

Rushdie's Mumbai

The Satanic Verses *was not a meditation on Islam,*
but about the author's faith in his own hometown

BY JYOTI THOTTAM/MUMBAI

AFTER FRIDAY PRAYERS ON FEB. 24, 1989, about 2,000 Muslims gathered at Mastan Talao, a public square in South Mumbai. They had gone there to protest the British government's decision to protect Salman Rushdie against the fatwa issued 10 days earlier by Ayatullah Ruhollah Khomeini, Iran's Supreme Leader. Khomeini had condemned Rushdie's novel, *The Satanic Verses,* as blasphemous to Islam and exhorted his followers to carry out a death sentence. Rushdie, who lived in London at the time, was given 24-hour police protection, and another round of protests began. The crowd in Mumbai, who carried banners reading I AM READY TO KILL RUSHDIE and RUSHDIE—RUSH+DIE, were unaware that the march's organizers had been arrested the night before by Indian authorities or that the protest itself had been banned. Instructed to end the march, the police moved in and arrested most of the protesters, but a small group broke away and continued down the main road. Just before reaching Crawford Market—a grand 19th century fruit and flower market—a line of policemen stopped them. There was a confrontation, and within an hour the police had fired scores of bullets, killing 11 people including two pilgrims on their way to Saudi Arabia, struck as they watched from a balcony nearby.

The furor over *The Satanic Verses* was one of those unsettling media experiences of the pre-Internet era in which images from distant corners of the globe seemed to coalesce into something bigger. A writer in London, rabid denunciations in Tehran, protests in South Africa and Pakistan, bookstores bombed in Berkeley. Mumbai (then called Bombay) was just one more angry city on the list. India lost more lives than any other country in the name of the fatwa, while the author himself survived almost a decade in hiding, publishing six books during his years undercover. *The Satanic Verses* is remembered 20 years later as part of a larger narrative about Iran vs. the West, but that is not the story Rushdie was trying to tell. *The Satanic Verses* was an attempt to engage in a conversation with India, and in particular with Mumbai, Rushdie's hometown, about whether its character as a multireligious yet secular society was strengthened or undermined by the expression of extreme, unpopular or unorthodox views. It is an argument that remains unresolved but is more urgent than ever.

Chaos Theory

BEFORE THE FATWA WAS EVER UTTERED, Rushdie spelled out what *The Satanic Verses* was trying to say. In a letter to then Indian Prime Minister Rajiv Gandhi in October 1988, protesting his decision to ban the book, Rushdie wrote: "Let's remember that the book isn't actually about Islam, but about migration, metamorphosis, divided selves, love, death, London and Bombay." Jihadist groups were practically unknown at the time in India, but Hindu nationalist parties—the Shiv Sena in Mumbai (they were responsible for renaming the city) and its national ally, the Bharatiya Janata Party (BJP)—were on the rise. Rushdie's response to their narrow view of a "Hindu India" was to write a book premised on the radical idea of an India broad enough to accommodate his florid, fantastical irreverence. Like Rushdie, his hero Saladin Chamcha (*chamcha* means flunky) was a Muslim only in the "lackadaisical, light manner of Bombayites." After years of living in London, Chamcha returns to Mumbai, electrified and confounded by what was once his home: "India; it jumbled things up."

Rushdie embraces that confusion. His India is a place where people are free to mix and match traditions, to satirize and discard them

63

**BITTER
OUTRAGE**
*Muslim
youth protest
Rushdie in
Birmingham,
England*

at will. As an Indian writer in London, Rushdie was the epitome of the cosmopolite—a world citizen—and that cosmopolitan vision comes to life in *The Satanic Verses*. The two protagonists, Chamcha and Gibreel Farishta (literally, Angel Gabriel), are both actors from Mumbai, one a British voice-over artist, the other a Bollywood superstar. They meet on a hijacked plane, magically survive its destruction and spend the rest of the novel circling back through their earlier lives. Both are psychologically damaged, and Farishta's delusions turn into the novel's controversial dream sequences, in which Rushdie reimagines the Prophet Muhammad's life. In the novel he is the Messenger, Mahound, in a place called Jahilia: "There is a god here called Allah (means simply, the god). Ask the Jahilians and they'll acknowledge that this fellow has some sort of overall authority, but he isn't very popular: an all-rounder in an age of specialist statues." The novel lurches back and forth between dream life and real life, and the two heroes eventually return to Mumbai.

The historical and religious allusions, Bollywood in-jokes and references to Indian politics made the book difficult reading, but they were essential to its vitality. E.M. Forster found something vaguely disturbing about the emerging cosmopolitanism of the early 20th century. "London was but a foretaste of this nomadic civilization which is altering human nature so profoundly, and throws upon personal relations a stress greater than they have ever borne before," he wrote in *Howard's End*. Rushdie revels in this strange new world. In the opening scene of *The Satanic Verses,* his heroes fall out of the sky and, thus completely unmoored, are reborn. "*The Satanic Verses* celebrates hybridity, impurity, intermingling, the transformation that comes of new and unexpected combinations of human beings, cultures, ideas, politics, movies, songs," Rushdie wrote in a 1990 essay. "It rejoices in mongrelization and fears the absolutism of the Pure."

Mumbai, for Rushdie, was London's mongrel twin. "I had a Christian ayah (nanny), for whom at Christmas we would put up a tree and sing carols about baby Jesus without feeling in the least ill-at-ease," Rushdie wrote in 1985. "My friends were Hindus, Sikhs, Parsis, and none of this struck me as being particularly important." Nostalgia for that life permeates *The Satanic Verses,* which looks back at Mumbai with the trembling infatuation of the long-gone returned.

Narrow and Narrower

SUBHASH DESAI REMEMBERS A VERY DIFferent Mumbai. He grew up in the 1950s in a neighborhood built around a former cotton mill on the far outskirts of the city. "On the eastern part, there was a creek, there were mangroves," Desai says.

Weekends meant a trip into town to the beach at Juhu or Chowpatty. The traders and merchants who built the city gave way to industrialists and small manufacturing, attracting millions of migrant laborers seeking jobs. In 1961, the population was 4.1 million; since then it has quadrupled. Desai, a leader of the Shiv Sena, represents the suburb of Goregaon in the state assembly and supports closing Mumbai to new migrants. "People mindlessly continued to come here and settle," without any thought to where they would live or how they would get water or electricity, he says. "The city has virtually collapsed."

Rushdie wrote *The Satanic Verses* just as the Shiv Sena was coming into its first flush of power, having successfully yoked its original nativist message—reserving jobs and housing for locals—to the BJP's Hindu nationalism. In 1989, the Shiv Sena won its first seat in Parliament, and the BJP won 85, the first time the two parties made a significant national impact. Rushdie satirizes the Hindu right throughout *The Satanic Verses,* as well as in his later books, holding up his gorgeous hybrid city as an alternative. Desai dismisses that notion as fantasy. The sophisticated, glamorous city of Rushdie's imagination, he says, exists only in the posh high-rises of its southern tip. "There only Salman Rushdie's dream of sweet Mumbai can be seen."

For Muslims who do not belong to Rushdie's South Mumbai élite, the alternative to Hindu nationalist orthodoxy is not Rushdie's openness. It is India's inclusive, essentially conservative ideal, in which every community has the space to follow its own traditions, but the price of that freedom is the responsibility not to offend. That is why *The Satanic Verses* was rejected by the Muslims of Mumbai, who otherwise had little in common with the extreme views of Iran's ayatullahs. They had a different notion of cosmopolitanism, in which the freedom of the individual was less important than what bound communities into one harmonious whole.

Back to the Future

THAT EMPHASIS ON ACCOMMODATION, ON getting along, makes the 1989 violence in Mumbai even more baffling. The full story of what happened that day is not widely known, but it is well told in an April 1989 report by the Committee for the Protection of Democratic Rights, a panel of lawyers, academics and journalists. None of the large, established Muslim civic organizations in the city supported the Feb. 24 protest march, and those who did protest actually agreed with the Indian government's ban on the book. Their anger was directed at Rushdie and Britain, not at the Indian authorities. "The police acted wrongly at every turn," the committee concluded, substituting force for common sense and good communication. "The entire incident left the Muslims extremely bitter with the government, the police and with their established leaders."

Their bitterness has only worsened over time. "The perception is there of discrimination by the police," says Sheikh Mateen, the general secretary of Jamaat-e-Islami Hind in Maharashtra, a proudly secular social-service group founded in 1941. Young Muslim men in Mumbai complain that they are constantly harassed by the police, he says, creating a toxic cycle of suspicion and distrust between them. The sense of being targeted by the state fuels the anger of the small minority of Indian Muslims who are radicalized, Mateen says. "If there is no justice, then there is frustration." After the Mumbai terrorist attacks of November 2008, concern about the marginalization and radicalization of Indian Muslims briefly resurfaced. But once that attack was linked to Pakistan, India turned its attention elsewhere.

Perhaps the greatest irony of the controversy is that India is both more and less open to the book than it was 20 years ago. *The Satanic Verses* is freely available in India. But the book remains officially banned, and India's political support for free expression remains limited. Taslima Nasreen, a writer who took refuge in India when she was threatened in her native Bangladesh, was forced to leave in 2008; the Indian artist M.F. Husain has lived in exile for years, denounced by the Hindu nationalist right wing for his nude paintings of gods and goddesses. "It seems like these days India has lost sight of the fact that it's important to defend these imaginative freedoms," Rushdie said in a 2008 interview with the novelist Rana Dasgupta in Kolkata's *Telegraph* newspaper. "Without that, all this kind of modernizing, job-creating, triumphal India really doesn't mean anything." Rushdie, like so many outsiders to India, assumed that the country would pick up cosmopolitanism as easily as it did the imported soaps and chocolates now sold in Crawford Market. It didn't happen. In that sense, E.M. Forster's London is as distant from Salman Rushdie's Mumbai as ever. ∎

A Rush to Death

In an old British soccer stadium, 96 fans died tragically—and the modern, global game was born

By Adam Smith/Sheffield

B Y THE 1980S, ENGLISH SOCCER had become a global byword for horror—a window on a society at its most vicious and divided. Violent hooligans, a scourge since the 1960s, had begun to define the game, as fans fought inside and outside stadiums. English teams had been exiled from European competition in 1985 after a charge by Liverpool fans before the European Cup final in Belgium left 39 supporters dead, most of them fans of the Italian club Juventus.

Those fans who went to games not looking for a fight were treated as if they were. The family-friendly comforts of sports stadiums in the U.S. were unknown. Met by police at railway stations, fans were herded into caged sections of dilapidated stadiums, where most of them had to stand to watch a game. Basic amenities were so lacking that people urinated right there on the crumbling terraces. The stadiums were death traps, and everyone knew it. In 1985, a blaze begun accidentally in an antiquated stadium in Bradford, northern England, claimed 56 lives. Attendances were dwindling. At just the time that U.S. sports were turning themselves into spectacles that could appeal to all ages, both sexes and any income group, English soccer was becoming the preserve of those who had the fortitude to put up with a couple of hours of discomfort, while risking being punched in the face for the privilege. "The game," says John Williams, a specialist in the sociology of soccer at the University of Leicester, England, "was in a very difficult place."

It would get worse. On April 15, 1989, more than 50,000 fans of Liverpool and Nottingham Forest followed their teams to a semifinal of the FA Cup, soccer's oldest competition, that would be played on neutral ground at the Hillsborough stadium in Sheffield, a town in Northern England. When too many Liverpool fans were directed into fenced pens at one end of the ground, a crush soon developed. Hundreds more streamed in after police opened the gates to let in those waiting outside. From within the pens, people cried out for help. Others screamed. But conditioned by the endemic violence at games to look out for threats to public order and not to public safety, police were slow to respond. When a narrow gate sprang open in the terrace's perimeter fence—the fences had been put up at many stadiums to stymie invasions of the field—officers pushed back those desperately trying to escape, and closed it.

Five and a half minutes after kickoff, the game was halted. By then, though, bodies were piled close to the fence, many of them blue, eyes staring ahead, "a crowded, twisted vision of a rush to death as only a master of the age could paint it," U.S. novelist Don DeLillo wrote in his novel *Mao II*. Ninety-five Liverpool fans were killed in the disaster, virtually all by asphyxia; another, left comatose by the crush, would die in 1993. Trevor Hicks, who'd stood on the terraces a few meters from his two daughters, Sarah, 19, and Victoria, 15, found them lying side by side on the pitch. As a medic attended to the elder, Hicks tried desperately to clear vomit from Victoria's throat. Neither daughter survived. "We lost all our family," says Hicks. "It completely turned our lives upside down."

The day would have a similar effect on English—in fact, world—soccer. Lord Justice Peter Taylor, a senior British judge appointed by the government to investigate the tragedy and advise how to prevent a repeat, put it down largely to a "failure of police control." More importantly, Taylor took a knife to the "general malaise" afflicting the game, from its unsafe grounds and poor treatment of law-abiding fans to hooliganism. "Years of patching up grounds, of ... muddling through on a wing and a prayer must be over," he wrote in his final report. It was time, he said, for "higher standards both in bricks and mortar and in human relationships."

Taylor largely got his way. Following his recommendations, teams in the top two divisions

AFTERMATH
Hillsborough's Leppings Lane stand, where overcrowding caused scores of fans to be crushed to death

of English soccer converted their grounds to all-seater stadiums by the start of the 1994 season. That not only made game days safer, but, combined with better stewarding and the removal of fencing, also "had a major effect on hooliganism inside and around stadiums," says sociologist Williams. "The point [Taylor] made was that if you give people the sense that the environment of the stadium is defined by that kind of violence and aggressive behavior, then that's what you'll get," he adds.

Other changes followed. The better, safer facilities Taylor demanded fed the top clubs' plans to reach a wider audience and boost earnings. That, and the need to recover the costs of converting their stadiums, would soon help push 22 clubs to break away from the old structure and launch the English Premier League (EPL)—and alter the face of world sport. On the back of TV revenue—Sky, the satellite-TV broadcaster owned by Rupert Murdoch, now pays $700 million a season to broadcast games in Britain—the EPL has become the richest soccer league in the world, and of all sports leagues is the one that does best outside its home market. EPL games are broadcast live in Asia, where team shirts of Manchester United and Liverpool, Chelsea and Arsenal are a fashion staple from Shanghai to Mumbai. For the 2009-10 season, sports powerhouse ESPN shares rights to broadcast games in the U.S., a sure sign that the EPL is now one of the global big leagues.

For those able to remember standing in the rotting stadiums of old, the Premier League's swish arenas stand as the disaster's most powerful legacy. None is as striking as the Emirates Stadium, the home of Arsenal, a leading London club. Opened in 2006 at a cost of around $600 million—selling the naming rights to the Dubai-based airline recouped about a quarter of that—the stadium is the closest thing there is to the perfect, simulated backdrop you find on a computer game. Catering to one of the sport's most affluent fan bases, the wide concourses are replete with comfortable places to eat. In the stands, seats "have improved the comfort, and the view's much better," says Frank Rossi, a local antiques trader who watched his first Arsenal game in 1965.

Not everything has changed. At Hillsborough, much of the Carlsberg West Stand, as the Leppings Lane end is now known, remains pretty much as it was in 1989. The narrow tunnel, into which so many Liverpool fans were crammed on their way to the terrace, now offers access to its seats. One afternoon in late April 2009, much of the first two rows were still taken up with floral tributes laid to mark the recent anniversary. Many were wilting. But on the edge of the field of play, close to where so many perished on that dreadful Saturday afternoon in 1989, small yellow flowers had sprung from the turf. Out of darkness, a brighter future. ∎

After The Bubble

Japan's economy has been in the doldrums for so long that it's hard to imagine the time when conspicuous consumption was the order of the day

BY BILL POWELL/TOKYO

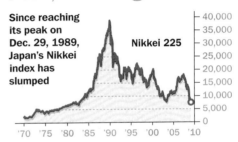

Peak, and Troughs

Since reaching
its peak on
Dec. 29, 1989,
Japan's Nikkei
index has
slumped

Nikkei 225

40,000
35,000
30,000
25,000
20,000
15,000
10,000
5,000
0

'70 '75 '80 '85 '90 '95 '00 '05 '10

Source: Yahoo! Finance

I N THE AUTUMN OF 1989, JIN MATSUSHITA was making more money than he ever dreamed he would; more money, indeed, than he thought he'd ever need. After joining Yamaichi Securities straight out of high school, Matsushita had worked his way up from lowly office boy scribbling stock prices on a chalkboard to fully fledged stockbroker in Yamaichi's nationwide army of salesmen—and what a golden time it was to be trading stocks for one of Japan's largest securities firms. Japanese companies like Toyota and Sony were becoming globally dominant, while the country's businessmen, flush with cash, fanned out across the world, snatching up iconic properties like New York City's Rockefeller Center, the fabled Pebble Beach golf course and Hollywood's Columbia Pictures. Matsushita himself was earning an annual salary of $150,000 plus a bonus that often exceeded his base pay. Everyone was getting rich. The Nikkei 225 stock index soared to an all-time high of 38,916 on Dec. 29, 1989. "It was a kind of miracle, I suppose," says Matsushita.

A TIRED MOOD *The scene today at Tokyo's Chiyoda commercial district*

REUTERS/CORBIS

FROM HIGH TO LOW *A boisterous 1989 scene at the Tokyo Stock Exchange*

It was the kind of miracle that doesn't last: an economic bubble that soon burst. What followed was collapse and years of torpor that came to be known as Japan's "lost decade." Neither Tokyo property prices nor Japanese stocks—nor the Japanese people, for that matter—have ever fully recovered. The Nikkei index on Aug. 31, 2009, closed at 10,492, an astonishing 73% below its 1989 peak. And Matsushita, now 73, is working the night shift at a convenience store just to make ends meet.

Looking back, it's odd that so few people saw the bust coming. I certainly didn't. In 1989, I was Tokyo bureau chief for *Newsweek*, and I lived through the bubble years acutely aware of what strange days they were, yet without quite realizing those days were numbered. It should have been obvious that such excess was unsustainable. At one point, the combined value of Tokyo real estate was said to eclipse that of the entire U.S. In Japan you could easily

spend more than $1,000 on a round of golf or on an evening in a hostess bar in Ginza. All this reinforced the notion that Japan was an industrial giant that seemed able to outcompete even the mighty U.S. George H.W. Bush, then U.S. President, came to Japan with trade at the top of his agenda, only to famously throw up on Kiichi Miyazawa, Japan's Prime Minister, during a state dinner. Miyazawa gently cradled Bush's head as the stricken President slumped in his chair, an image that we journalists couldn't resist using as a metaphor. The country that had been vanquished militarily now seemed poised to conquer the world economically. The *Atlantic* captured the angst this caused in a two-part series entitled "Containing Japan."

Why did serious publications think Japan needed to be contained? Because at the time it seemed as if its politicians, policymakers and business leaders had patented a superior brand of capitalism. In less than two generations, the country had climbed out of the wreckage of war to become the world's second largest economy. Books like *Japan as Number One* detailed how different its economic system was from that of the laissez-faire U.S.—the government directed capital into key industries and allowed powerful business groups, called *keiretsu,* to exclude competitors from domestic markets, while Japanese companies made relentless inroads into Western markets. Americans who once scared themselves silly watching news footage of phalanxes of Soviet troops parading through Red Square instead made themselves queasy by watching phalanxes of Toyota workers performing calisthenics before hitting the factory floor.

Technology and money and power were flowing across the Pacific to Japan, and salarymen—guys like Jin Matsushita—were among the lucky beneficiaries. Tokyo in those days was a gilded city, where restaurants sold sushi sprinkled with gold flakes. Other foreign correspondents would cover wars and risk getting shot. In Tokyo, as the dollar sank in value against the yen, the greatest risk I faced was having a heart attack when the bill for dinner arrived.

Japan was exotic, and it could also be insular and xenophobic. When foreigners stayed out past midnight, after the subways in Tokyo closed, they risked being unable to get a cab home. I was once out carousing into the morning hours with a couple of friends from Japan's Ministry of Finance—the élite among Japan's powerful bureaucrats—when we tried to flag a taxi. I told my friends no driver would stop unless I hid in the shadow of a nearby building. "No, that's not true," one of them protested. I hid, and within seconds a cab pulled up for my Japanese companions. I jumped into the backseat, much to the dismay of the cabbie. My buddy expressed shock. "What a racist country we are," he muttered. I laughed. This wasn't racism, it was capitalism. Cab drivers assumed a foreigner wasn't going very far, whereas the average salaryman lived some distance from the center of town, guaranteeing a big fare. Like everything during the bubble, it was all about the money.

The Toll of a Long Slumber

BUBBLES ARE FUN, BUT WHEN JAPAN'S IMploded, it sucked the life out of an entire country, stripped it of ambition and of the sense of rapid progress that had come to define its postwar history. Yoichi Funabashi, now the editor of the *Asahi Shimbun,* one of Japan's most influential daily newspapers, told me: "An entire generation has been born and grown up, and known nothing but slow economic growth and limited opportunity. Compare them to their fathers' generation, the generation that turned so many Japanese companies into household names all over the world. I don't think young people today have any idea what they are going to do, or what even they are supposed to be doing."

On a visit to Tokyo today, it's easy to miss this toll that the country's long slumber has taken. The city has always been orderly and efficient, and parts of it now seem even more prosperous than they did in 1989. The once drab business district around Tokyo Station near the Imperial Palace is now full of high-end retail shops and pleasant pedestrian malls. Japan in some ways managed to spread the economic pain over 20 years, so that it is more like an endless dull ache than an open wound.

For many Japanese, though, the pain is not merely abstract and psychological. Consider Matsushita. Nine years after the Nikkei peaked, Yamaichi Securities—the company where Matsushita, in true Japanese fashion, spent his entire career—went under. It had finally succumbed to the moribund stock market, as well as a scandal in which company officials got

CAREFREE NIGHTS
Businessmen are entertained by a hostess at a Hiroshima bar in 1989

71

THE COST OF EXCESS *Jin Matsushita, now 73, has seen far better days*

caught hiding trading losses. Matsushita had 90% of his life savings tied up in Yamaichi stock when it imploded. Although he was a financial adviser and ought to have understood the risk, this is not so surprising. Ask an American what he does for a living, and he'll usually describe his profession: I'm a banker, an engineer, an auto worker. Ask a Japanese, and he'll name his employer—I work for Toyota, I work for Sony— because he fiercely identifies with that organization. When I gently suggest to Matsushita that perhaps it was unwise for him to have put all his savings in one basket, he gets a bit defensive. "My wife and I had furious squabbles over this after Yamaichi went down," he says quietly. "She asked how I could do this. But I worked for Yamaichi Securities," he explains.

"It never occurred to me, never, that one day our company would not exist." And then, to reinforce his point, he says to his American visitor: "One year ago, did you think it was possible for General Motors to go bankrupt?"

I don't have the heart to tell him yes. Americans today are learning only too well that industrial icons can fail when a bubble bursts. The crash of the debt-fueled U.S. real estate market and the subsequent financial crisis plunged the country into the worst recession in decades. Although the U.S. is starting to show signs of stability, Japan's postbubble malaise demonstrates how long it can take for a damaged financial system to heal.

Twenty years on, Matsushita is still counting the costs of Japan's years of excess. Sitting

AN ERA OF NEED *Meals are distributed by a soup kitchen in Tokyo's Sumida River*

in the community room of a residential complex east of Tokyo, where he now lives, he explains how he bought his apartment in 1996, the year he retired from Yamaichi. He paid 76 million yen (about $775,000 at current exchange rates) for the place, borrowing 59 million yen to finance it. That debt is the bane of Matsushita's existence. When Yamaichi failed in 1998, wiping out most of his savings, he had no way to pay off the note with just his meager income from social security. The price of his apartment collapsed soon after he had bought it, so he can't sell. And unlike in the U.S., where owners can take their lumps and walk away from mortgages without the debt following them, Matsushita's is a "recourse" loan—common in Japan—which means that harsh penalties

await those who fail to keep making payments for any reason.

So eight years ago, Matsushita took a job at a local 24-hour convenience store to make enough money to live and pay off his mortgage. The septuagenarian works the graveyard shift—9:45 p.m. to 7:15 a.m.—for $81 a day. "I usually do get to work overtime hours and make a bit more money," he says, "because the high school and college kids [who relieve him in the morning] aren't very responsible. They are always coming up with excuses as to why they can't make it in until 10 a.m. or so." And just before heading off for another night shift, he adds: "That never happened when I was young." But when Matsushita was young, Japan had its best days ahead of it. ■

WEB SLINGER
*Berners-Lee is creating
the next-generation Net*

The Net's Big Bang

Tim Berners-Lee created the Web—and made the Internet a mass medium

BY VINTON CERF

I GREW UP READING TOM SWIFT JR. stories. Looking back at the story of the Web makes me think it should be titled something like *Tim Berners-Lee and his World Wide Web Machine.* When Tim began his work with Robert Cailliau in 1989 at CERN, Europe's particle-physics lab in Geneva, the Internet was just beginning to emerge as a commercially available service. But it lacked standardized systems for formatting, storing, locating and retrieving information.

Tim solved these problems by writing Hypertext Transfer Protocol (HTTP), a computer language for communicating documents over the Internet, and by designing a system to give documents addresses. He also created the first browser—calling it the World-WideWeb—as well as a language (Hypertext Markup Language, or HTML) for creating Web pages and the first server software allowing those pages to be stored and accessed by others.

Like many people, I was completely unaware at the time of these historic developments. The Web first came to my attention in early 1993 when Marc Andreessen and Eric Bina released their graphical browser called Mosaic. It is hard to evoke the stunning impact Mosaic had on the community of Internauts who until that time were accustomed to text-based tools and keyboard navigation for retrieving content. The addition of imagery and magazine-like layout transformed the Internet into a gigantic publishing vehicle, an information-creation engine.

Web users could interact with information in ways no book, radio, television or newspaper could offer

It was as if a new guild based on new technology had been created in the Middle Ages; virtually every medium that had been invented in the past could now be presented through the Internet and users could interact with this information in ways no book, radio, television or newspaper could offer. The tsunami that flowed into the Internet via the World Wide Web also created the need for tools to find specific content in an ocean full of information. Thus were born a series of search engines and the giant companies such as Google and Yahoo! associated with them.

As with many inventions, once the conditions for their invention have been satisfied, many variations on a theme will emerge to interact, compete and evolve in a new universe. And like many other inventors I have known, Tim (now Sir Tim) is modest, passionate and committed to the further evolution of this universe. As the head of the World Wide Web Consortium at MIT, he continues to develop new capabilities for the Web. His passion these days is to find a way to reveal the content of huge databases on the Internet that are otherwise not visible to the search engines of today. This search for the Semantic Web has the potential to be even more significant than his invention of the World Wide Web. His success could open a new chapter in the history of information technology. ∎

Cerf, known as one of the fathers of the Internet, is chief Internet evangelist at Google

Mimicking the Sun

*Touted as a miracle of energy, cold fusion served
only to create confusion and division*

By Eben Harrell

PHILIPPE PLAILLY—EURELIOS/SCIENCE PHOTO LIBRARY

Dynamic duo
*Pons (right) and
Fleischmann sparked a
scientific controversy*

W**HEN A SCIENTIFIC DIS**-covery is billed as "right up there with fire, the cultivation of plants, and with electricity," it had better be pretty good. That's how Chase Peterson, the president of the University of Utah, sold an experiment by two chemists working at his institution, B. Stanley Pons and Martin Fleischmann, on March 23, 1989. It was, sadly, a bust—one that set off a chain reaction in American scientific circles.

Nuclear fusion, the phenomenon that makes the sun burn, occurs when two atoms fuse together and release energy. The laws of physics—so everyone thought—held that it was impossible to sustain a fusion reaction, even briefly, without subjecting atomic nuclei to the kind of extreme temperatures and pressures found inside the sun or a thermonuclear bomb. But Pons and Fleischmann claimed to have achieved cold fusion at room temperature. By placing two metal electrodes into a beaker of water filled with the ions of deuterium (heavy hydrogen), the scientists said they had forced the ions to fuse to form helium, liberating large amounts of heat.

The discovery promised a cheap, almost inexhaustible supply of energy. All you needed to do, Fleischmann and Pons claimed of their rudimentary apparatus, was fill it up and plug it in.

When physicists pointed out that their claim was impossible, a culture war broke out. Chemists accused physicists of being territorial and jealously protecting their claim to fusion-research grants. At a special session of the American Chemical Society on April 12, Pons received a rapturous ovation. Shortly after,

Within a few months, a 22-member federal panel laid out numerous problems with the experiment

he told TIME that "chemists are supposed to discover chemicals. The physicists don't like it when they discover physicals."

The physicists didn't take that lying down. Some at MIT examined footage from a Utah TV station, freezing a frame that included Pons and Fleischmann's findings. When they ran calculations off this screen grab, they found several errors. At a meeting of the American Physical Society in Baltimore on May 1 (Pons and Fleischmann were not present), Steven Koonin of the California Institute of Technology summed up the mood: "We're suffering from the incompetence and, perhaps, delusion of Professors Pons and Fleischmann."

The public and media weren't sure whom to believe. Fleischmann had earlier discovered a photon-scattering effect that physicists had failed to predict, leading some commentators to accuse élite coastal institutions of trying to tear down pioneering researchers in the heartland. "It became a red-state, blue-state thing," says Charles Seife, author of *Sun in a Bottle,* the definitive account of the history of fusion.

Within a few months of the announcement, a 22-member federal panel of scientists laid out numerous problems with the Pons-Fleischmann experiment. Other researchers were unable to reproduce the pair's results, and Pons and Fleischmann faded into obscurity. But the allure of their "beautiful idea" survives. To this day, a small but dedicated number continue to work on cold fusion despite the evidence that it is impossible.

It would be nice to think that you could power the world from a beaker of water. But sadly, that's closer to alchemy than science. ∎

AT THAT TIME

"Any scientist who managed to harness fusion would be guaranteed a Nobel Prize for Physics, untold riches from licensing the process and a place in history alongside Einstein and slightly above Edison. Any scientist who confirmed the claim would get part of the resulting avalanche of research dollars, and anyone who shot it down would gain acclaim within the scientific community."
—From TIME's May 8, 1989, cover story

A Triumph For Love

*When Denmark became the first
country to legalize gay unions,
it provided a model of tolerance
for the rest of the world to follow*

By Lisa Abend/Copenhagen

Axel Axgil, 94, holds a picture of himself with his now deceased husband, Eigil. They were the world's first legally united gay couple

IN THE PHOTOGRAPH, THE AXGILS radiate pure joy. Newly married, they lean into each other across the seat of the horse-drawn carriage, their hands clutching glasses of champagne, their lips locked in an ecstatic kiss. The crowd swirling around them in front of Copenhagen's town hall could pass for a regular group of wedding guests, if it weren't for the boom mikes jutting over their heads. That horde of reporters and cameramen is what gives it away: the pair in the photo are no ordinary newly-weds. It was Oct. 1, 1989, and, dressed in matching suits, Axel and Eigil Axgil had just become the first gay couple in the world to legalize their union.

Today, that photograph hangs on the wall of 94-year-old Axel's cozy Copenhagen apartment, amid a crop of houseplants and ceramic tchotch-kes. His husband, Eigil, has been dead for 14 years, but Axel still remembers the wedding as if it were yesterday: the stream of gifts that began arriving early that sunny Sunday morning, the taxi ride to the town hall, the asparagus soup they ate at the reception. More than anything, he remembers the crowd. "I'd never seen so many television cameras. There were journalists there from all over the world," he says. "It wasn't until that moment that we realized the historic significance of what we were doing."

Twenty years later, the relative ease with which Denmark enacted that historic moment remains striking. Seven countries now permit same-sex marriage, and 15 more authorize civil unions. (Some states in Australia, Argentina and Mexico also recognize civil partnerships. Five U.S. states have approved full marriage equality for gay couples.) But in most cases, legislation has been bitterly contentious—witness the 2005 mass protests staged by conservative groups in Spain, or California's November 2008 referendum over-turning marriage equality. In Denmark, where polls from the time showed only 25% of the public opposed it, the landmark civil-unions bill passed on May 26, 1989, with a clear majority. Steffen Jensen, of the Danish National Association of Gays and Lesbians, remembers the moment as re-markably moving. "The Danish Parliament isn't like the British one—there's never any shouting or clapping; we're very reserved," he says. "But when the law passed, everyone in the audience rose and bowed to the legislators."

What made Denmark so receptive to gay mar-riage so early? It's not as though the Danes have a long history of tolerance toward homosexu-als. Three years after World War II, when Axel Lundahl-Madsen (he would later change his sur-name to Axgil, a combination of his and Eigil's given names) helped found the first Danish gay-rights organization, even the word *homosexual* was still taboo, which is why the group called itself the Association of '48. "When I came out, I lost my job as a bookkeeper. And my landlord kicked me out of my apartment," says Axgil.

It would be nearly 40 years before the Associa-tion of '48 could change its name to the National Association of Gays and Lesbians. Even then, bar-riers to equality remained: a 1984 attempt to le-galize same-sex unions was defeated in Parliament. Yet by the end of that decade, something had changed to make legalization seem the only logical option.

For many, that something was an epidemic. "AIDS did two things," says Jensen. "First, it made conservatives think that it might be good to support stable, monoga-mous relationships among gays. And second, it brought homosexuals into the public sphere. For the first time, politicians were actually meeting gay men and lesbian wom-en, and realizing they weren't any different from straight people." Tom Ahlberg, who, as deputy mayor of Copenhagen in 1989, married Axel and Eigil, agrees that AIDS was a significant factor, but sees its role somewhat differently. "Given the tragedy of what was happening, I think we as a so-ciety felt we owed something, some sign of sym-pathy and respect, to gays."

The legislation does not fully equate gay unions with straight ones. It prohibits homosexu-als from adopting children, for example, and re-fers to the sanctioned relationships as "registered partnerships" rather than marriages. But from the start, that distinction was blurred. Ahlberg spent the months after the legislation's approval working with gay activists to prepare for the first ceremony. "I wanted to acknowledge the historic

Till Death Do Us Part

According to a May 1997 article in *Psychology Today,* almost a decade after legalization the divorce rate among gay couples in Denmark was only 17%, compared to 46% for their married heterosexual counterparts.

> **'I think we as a society felt we owed something, some sign of sympathy and respect, to gays.'**
>
> —*Tom Ahlberg, former deputy mayor of Copenhagen*

THE BLUSH-ING GROOMS
Larsen, left, and Carlsen at the town hall in Copenhagen, where they were wed

significance of what was happening, but I also wanted to stick as closely as possible to the service for straight couples," he says.

In the end, Ahlberg changed almost nothing of the civil service, though he did make the unprecedented decision to open Copenhagen's town hall on a Sunday for the ceremony. Standing before 11 couples and their guests, Ahlberg gave a short speech that made only one alteration to the civil service—substituting the word *marriage* with the phrase *registered partnership*. He then led each couple, starting with Axel and Eigil, into a side room, where they exchanged their vows.

"It was totally wonderful," says Ove Carlsen, a psychologist who married minister Ivan Larsen that day. "There were musicians playing as we came down from the wedding room, and then we stepped out into the crowd, and everyone was cheering. At that moment, I knew we were writing history."

For the next few years, Axel and Eigil continued to run their gay-friendly bed and breakfast in northern Denmark. But decades of repression had left their mark: even after they married, each continued to refer to the other as his "friend." It wasn't until 1995 that Eigil, who lay in hospital suffering from the heart attack that would kill him, used the more accurate term. "A doctor saw I was always with him, and asked who I was," recounts Axgil. "And Eigil looked at me and said, 'Him? He's my husband.'"

Denmark still has a long way to go. Hate crimes against gays have risen in recent years. And activists are still working to achieve adoption rights and the right to wed in church for gay couples—to say nothing of the right to call their relationships marriages. "We were the first country to have legal partnerships, but all these other countries now have legal marriage," says Larsen. "I think, why are we so old-fashioned in Denmark?"

Yet despite the lag, Danish society is comfortable with the idea of same-sex unions. Since they were authorized, the country has witnessed some 4,700 gay and lesbian weddings. "There was never any negative reaction," says Ahlberg, who retired from office in 1994. "But Danes aren't given to controversy. That's why we call ourselves the consensus society."

For proof that gay marriage is now wholly a part of that consensus, you need only ask Kasper Jensen and Aedan Blanso. One afternoon in April, the two young men, who had been dating for five years, met up in front of the same town hall in which Axel and Eigil were married 20 years earlier. Both were born a few years before the registered-partnership legislation went into effect, so they are young enough to have fully absorbed its impact. "I grew up thinking that one day I would meet the right man, fall in love and get married," says Jensen. "You hear about these other countries where it's banned and it seems so sad. People should have the lives they want." ■

Animating Us

The Simpsons has reached cult status because it's really reality TV

By James Poniewozik

THERE ARE INDIE MOVIES, INDIE music and indie publishers. But because of the way the television business worked—series produced for millions of dollars to reach millions of people—there was never much that you could call indie TV. Until *The Simpsons.*

I realize that is an absurd claim to make for one of the most popular television shows in history, produced by a mammoth multinational media company (Fox), which has generated billions of dollars in merchandising and licensing revenue. But before Springfield's most famous yellow-skinned residents came to rival ubiquitous corporate mascots like Mickey Mouse and Bugs Bunny, the Simpsons were an outgrowth of that most indie of art forms, the alternative comic.

Since the late 1970s, Matt Groening had been publishing *Life in Hell,* a bleakly wry comic about an existentially alienated rabbit named Binky. Veteran producer James L. Brooks asked Groening to adapt the strip as animated shorts in *The Tracey Ullman Show,* but he instead created a family based loosely on his childhood, representing himself as Bart (an anagram for *brat*).

When *The Simpsons* debuted on Dec. 17, 1989, it was an utterly familiar thing on TV: a sitcom about a middle-class family. (Its very first episode was one of TV's hoary fixtures: a Christmas special.) But it quickly became clear that this was no *Cosby Show.*

Where classic sitcoms were essentially optimistic—in the end, father, mother, doctor, cop and teacher knew best—*The Simpsons* was set in a world where the authority figures were uniformly ridiculous. Bart's principal was an idiot, his teacher a bitter chain-smoker. His dad, Homer, was an incompetent technician at a nuclear power plant with an evil plutocrat for a boss; his TV idol, Krusty the Clown, a cynical hack peddling dangerous toys. No institution was safe: there was a jaded reverend, a doughnut-gobbling police chief, an ambulance-chasing lawyer and a stoner school-bus driver.

What allowed *The Simpsons* to cross over from alternative satire to mass hit was its likeable family and the vast world it built around them. Homer, Marge, Lisa, Bart and Maggie were a nuclear family in more ways than one, and not just because of Homer's job: they were the nucleus around which a vast cloud of satellite characters would revolve. As a cartoon, not limited by live actors and realism, *The Simpsons* had the freedom to go wherever and depict whomever it wanted, and it used this freedom to create a universe.

This meant that where its contemporary *Seinfeld* was "a show about nothing," *The Simpsons* was a show about everything. Through insufferably wholesome next-door neighbor Ned Flanders, the show became about religion. Through fatuous local news anchor Kent Brockman, it became about the media. Through Springfield's venal Mayor Quimby, it became about politics.

Above all, *The Simpsons* was a pop-culture phenomenon that was about pop culture itself. The show internalized the early criticism that it was a bad influence by creating the ultraviolent show-within-a-show *Itchy and Scratchy,* in which a homicidal mouse tormented a cat. It contained an entire fictional Hollywood: the Schwarzenegger-like action hero Rainier Wolfcastle, the superhero Radioactive Man (whose 1950s TV show was sponsored by Laramie cigarettes) and, of course, the fans, embodied in pudgy, fanatical Comic Book Guy, whose "worst episode ever" pronouncements echoed the show's own demanding critics.

That might explain why a show that was so specifically about America became the most popular TV export worldwide. Whether you lived in Springfield or Springbok, you could understand not just the universality of the family stories but the ubiquitous, disposable mass culture the show satirized.

The Simpsons' triumph is so absolute and its reach so total that it's hard to realize that there was a time when its dense, rapid-fire allusions weren't the lingua franca of comedy, when irreverence wasn't the default mode of popular culture. But its success was both a sea change and, in retrospect, a no-brainer: there is no one thing that unifies people more than the belief that they, like Matt Groening's funny-haired yellow wonders, are misfits. The world's biggest alternative entertainment turned TV inside out, by making outsiders in. ∎

He's Got Talent

Actor Hank Azaria *(Night at the Museum: Battle of the Smithsonian)* is the voice behind many *Simpsons* characters, including Moe the bartender, Apu the Kwik-E-Mart owner, Police Chief Wiggum, Professor Frink and Comic Book Guy.

Shock Snap

*How Robert Mapplethorpe's
strikingly explicit photographs
were on the front line of a
culture war that has yet to end*

By Richard Lacayo

THE SHOW WAS CALLED "THE Perfect Moment." It could just as well have been called "The Perfect Storm."

Twenty years ago, a traveling exhibition of photographs by Robert Mapplethorpe set off one of the fiercest episodes of America's "culture wars"—the enduring squabble over sexually explicit or sacrilegious art, leering pop music, raunchy TV comedies, radio shock jocks and every other sign of lewdness and irreverence in public life. Had he been around to see it, Mapplethorpe might have enjoyed the enormous fuss he had caused. But he had died in March 1989, at age 42, of complications from AIDS. By the time of his death, he was famous for three kinds of images: cool, rigorously conceived portraits and figure studies; sharply lit pictures of flowers; and photographs of gay S&M that left nothing to the imagination. Though he wasn't a fashion photographer, like Helmut Newton, Mapplethorpe trafficked in swank transgression. No less than his portraits and floral studies, his blunt images of rough sex—a man urinating into another man's mouth, a fist inserted just so into a man's anus—were serenely composed and luxuriously lit. The result may not always have expressed a perfect moment but it always presented a perfect paradox: a calm Apollonian framework for wild Dionysian content. And, like the Parthenon when it served as a powder keg for the Ottoman Turks, it was only a matter of time before it exploded.

Pictures of all three kinds were in "The Perfect Moment," though the S&M material was confined to an "X" portfolio that museums displayed in age-restricted cases or galleries. The show opened without incident in Philadelphia and moved from there to Chicago. The trouble started in the weeks leading to what was planned to be a July 1 opening at the Corcoran Gallery of Art in Washington, D.C.

A Political Backlash

AT THE TIME, CONSERVATIVES WERE ALready furious over *Piss Christ,* a photograph by Andres Serrano that showed a plastic crucifix immersed in a tank of what was said to be urine. What had them so angry was that Serrano had received a $15,000 grant from a North Carolina arts group that in turn had gotten money from the National Endowment for the Arts (NEA), the federal agency established in 1965 to subsidize artists and arts groups. In May, two Republican senators, Jesse Helms of North Carolina and Alfonse D'Amato of New York, denounced Serrano from the Senate floor, where D'Amato ripped to pieces the catalog of the show the picture had appeared in.

It wasn't long before Helms learned about the Mapplethorpe show, for which the NEA had provided $30,000 to the Philadelphia museum that had organized it. In June Helms sent around copies of the offending pictures to members of Congress. Soon more than 100 of them signed an angry letter to the NEA criticizing it for subsidizing a show that featured "morally repugnant materials of a sexual nature." The agency's defenders pointed to federal law that prohibited it from interfering with the content of the art it helped finance.

Although the Corcoran had gotten nothing from the NEA to subsidize its presentation of the Mapplethorpes, it received around $300,000 a year in federal funding. Concerned that a fight over the exhibit would just make things worse for the NEA—and that her museum could get caught up in the mess—the Corcoran's director, Christina Orr-Cahall, announced on June 12 that she was canceling the show. Now it was the turn of the art world to be outraged. Important Corcoran staffers resigned in protest. A group of angry Washington, D.C., artists projected pictures by Mapplethorpe onto the exterior of the museum. In the months that followed, Corcoran membership dropped 10%, and prominent artists including Ross Bleckner, Annette Lemieux and David Salle forbade the museum to exhibit their work. Meanwhile, the Mapplethorpe exhibition was picked up by another venue in the capital, the Washington Project for the Arts, where it was seen by nearly 50,000 people in less than a month.

All this proved too much for the Corcoran's board of trustees. Though they had originally supported the cancellation, now they began backing away. Orr-Cahall, who had joined the Corcoran just a few months earlier, was left stranded. By December, having concluded that the cancellation was a mistake—"We should have damned the torpedoes," she said, "and gone full speed ahead"—she resigned.

A few months later, the Mapplethorpe bomb would go off again. The show traveled to the Contemporary Arts Center (CAC) in Cincinnati, Ohio. As soon as it arrived, police shut it down briefly so they could videotape the pictures. Those tapes would be used as evidence in the criminal trial of CAC director Dennis Barrie, who would find himself and his museum charged with obscenity in connection with seven Mapplethorpe photographs, five showing sadomasochistic sex and two portraits of naked children.

The Cincinnati exhibition quickly reopened and eventually played to 80,000 visitors, but by September 1990 Barrie was in court, facing up to a year in jail. The eight-member jury, four men and four women, were mostly blue-collar and suburban. Only three had ever been to a museum. Prosecutors were so confident that they would agree that Mapplethorpe's pictures were obscene that the only witnesses they called were police officers brought in to testify that the photographs had actually been in the show.

Taste Test

THE STRATEGY BACKFIRED. FOR FIVE DAYS the defense called a multitude of museum directors, critics and other experts to testify. (This led to some priceless moments, like when the Philadelphia curator who had organized the show explained how meticulously Mapplethorpe had positioned the wrist that was penetrating a man's anus.) But the larger argument—that however shocking some of them might be, the pictures could be considered as art—was sound and it worked. After just two hours of jury deliberation, Barrie and the museum were acquitted.

After that, "The Perfect Moment" was over, but the conservative war on the NEA was not. For years the NEA struggled to placate its critics. It established a review board to look into any complaints about work it funded. It required its beneficiaries to sign a pledge promising not to produce obscene art. But none of this appeased Republicans in Congress. After the GOP electoral sweep in 1994, they tried to abolish the agency altogether. When that failed, they cut its funding by more than a third. Artists angry about the NEA decency requirements took their grievances to federal courts, which more than once found the requirements unconstitutionally vague.

Fights about government support for obscene art are rare these days and for an obvious reason: the government is a lot more careful about what it underwrites. After George W. Bush arrived at the White House, NEA funding started a slow climb back. President Barack Obama's first budget proposed to give the endowment $161.3 million. That figure, astonishingly, is still almost $8 million less than the agency got in 1989. Make no mistake, the battle over Mapplethorpe resulted in sustained harm to arts funding in the U.S. It was a perfect mess with a long, dismal aftermath. ■

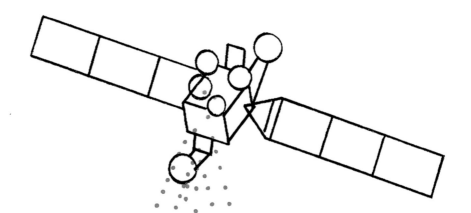

In Search Of Ourselves

GPS can find practically any person, place or thing. How on earth did we live without it?

By Andrew Marshall

A T 6:30 P.M. ON VALENTINE'S Day, 1989, a Delta rocket blasted off from Cape Canaveral and shot through the Florida twilight carrying a satellite prosaically known as Space Vehicle Number 14. Weighing roughly the same as a family car, and destined for an orbit of more than 12,000 miles (19,000 km) above our planet, the satellite was the first in a constellation of 24 making up the global positioning system (GPS). Along with the Internet, GPS is one of the great enabling technologies of our globalized age, and we have only begun to mine its seemingly limitless applications.

Developed by the U.S. Department of Defense—it had tested Navstar satellites as early as 1978—GPS is a sophisticated system that does something very simple: it establishes, with great accuracy, your position on earth. The satellites emit continuous radio signals that receivers translate into longitude, latitude, altitude, speed and time. Five years after SVN 14's launch, Navstar GPS—to use its official name—became fully operational at a cost of $12 billion in American taxpayers' money.

GPS can quickly locate my tent amid a field of mud, but it also abolishes a rite of passage: getting serendipitously lost

What a bargain. Operated by the 50th Space Wing at Schriever Air Force Base in Colorado, GPS started out by transforming modern warfare. Its satellites guided U.S. troops through sandstorms during Desert Storm in 1991 and the missiles used to "shock and awe" Baghdad in 2003. Today, almost everyone in a modern army—fighter pilots, tank crews, quartermasters—uses the technology. An emerging generation of commanders might struggle to imagine how wars were ever successfully waged without it.

Navstar GPS was designated as dual-use, a military technology also offered free to civilians. But for years, the Department of Defense deliberately degraded the signals to render them less accurate for nonmilitary purposes. Since 2000, when this policy was scrapped, GPS has gone from being a futuristic technology reserved for the U.S. military and Hollywood fantasists, to near ubiquity—from dual-use to omni-use.

GPS can be used to make maps, survey land, search and rescue, hunt for treasure, arrange car pools, track endangered species, monitor oil spills and—by shutting down her phone above a certain speed—stop your teenage daughter from texting while driving the family car. Greenpeace has used GPS receivers to expose the illegal trade in electronic waste from Britain to Nigeria. A British company has found a way to use GPS-enabled cell phones to calculate your carbon footprint.

Europe is developing a GPS system called Galileo. China is investing in Galileo and, in April, launched the second satellite in a constellation that will one day rival it. Russia's Soviet-era GLONASS system, restored with the help of India's space agency, plans to go global. In 2008 then Russian Defense Minister Sergei Ivanov gave Prime Minister Vladimir Putin a GLONASS-enabled collar for his Labrador Koni. "She looks sad," Ivanov reportedly said, after Putin had put the collar around his dog's neck. "[Her] free life is over." Koni's owner disagreed. "She's wagging her tail," said Putin. "That means she likes it."

Not all of us are wagging our tails. In 2006, the Australian Privacy Foundation gave a Big Brother Award to a junk-mail company that used GPS units to track its delivery staff. The following year, thousands of New York City taxi drivers went on strike to protest plans to put similar units in every cab, which some drivers felt was an invasion of privacy. (The plans went ahead anyway.) The Egyptian government is so worried about giving a technological aid to terrorists that it has banned all GPS-enabled devices. When the iPhone debuted in Cairo in 2009, it was without its navigation feature.

GPS has changed our lives for better and worse. A cell phone can quickly locate my tent amid a field of mud at a rock festival, but it also abolishes a rite of passage: getting serendipitously lost there. Strapping a GPS-enabled watch to my son's wrist might bring me peace of mind, but it will do nothing to make the streets safer for our children. On a planet of 6.7 billion souls, GPS helps us to find ourselves. But it sometimes dazzles us so much that we forget what we still seek. ∎

Hunting Ground

Millions of GPS-armed adventurers participate in a game called geocaching, seeking over 800,000 individual caches secreted in outdoor hideaways all over the world.

Black Gold On the Last Frontier

Americans were outraged when the Alaskan wilderness was fouled by millions of gallons of crude spilled by the tanker Exxon Valdez. Years later, the U.S. is still weighing the environmental costs of oil development

By Bryan Walsh/Prince William Sound

TRACKS ON THE TUNDRA
A pipeline zigzags across a North Slope oil field in the Alaskan Arctic

MANDY LINDBERG KNEELS down on the stony beach on Knight Island, in Alaska's Prince William Sound, and begins digging. The land around her is some of the most beautiful in the U.S. Snow-capped mountains, their flanks lush with hemlock and spruce, thrust out of the glacier-fed waters of the sound. Pale Arctic terns and endangered Kittlitz's murrelets skim the etched shoreline. To the northwest, fishing boats are setting out their gill nets, readying for the sockeye salmon's run. But as she turns her shovel on the beach, Lindberg uncovers a scar on the sound's seemingly pristine face: a pool of watery crude oil, chemical sheen glistening, fills in the hole. Search elsewhere on the beach, and on other islands in the sound, and you'll find more, just beneath the surface. The oil is the last remnant of the crude spilled on March 24, 1989, by a tanker named *Exxon Valdez* that ran aground just after midnight while on its way out to sea with 53 million gallons (200 million liters) of Alaskan oil on board; according to scientists from the National Oceanic and Atmospheric Administration (NOAA), about 20,000 gallons (76,000 liters) still remain buried on beaches around the sound. "At the initial time of the cleanup, we really thought this would be a one-shot deal," says Jeep Rice, the NOAA scientist who led the study, as he stands on the beach, which was nicknamed

VANISHING CULTURE *Seal-hunting, an Inupiat way of life, is threatened by melting ice*

Death Marsh during the cleanup. "We had no idea there would be lingering oil."

Then again, a lot of oil—and a lot of printer's ink—was spilled because of the accident. The *Exxon Valdez* was at the time considered to be the worst man-made environmental disaster in U.S. history, and news of it reverberated around the world. America's last true wilderness had been violated. At least 11 million gallons (42 million liters) of crude bled into the water when the tanker struck Bligh Reef near the port town of Valdez, the terminus of the Trans-Alaska Pipeline. For months after the grounding, large swaths of the sound and its islands were coated with a foul layer of crude. Hundreds of thousands of shorebirds were killed within weeks; a productive fishing industry was damaged for years. Americans were horrified by images of oil-covered sea otters and other wildlife. A New York judge compared the spill to Hiroshima; the captain of the *Exxon Valdez*, Joseph Hazelwood, who was not in the wheelhouse at the time of the accident, was tried on felony charges (he ultimately was convicted of a misdemeanor and fined $50,000). "It was a bad, bad time," says Stan Stephens, a veteran tour-boat operator in Valdez. "People can't even talk about it without getting emotional."

LUCIAN READ—RAPPORT PRESS

the Prince William Sound disaster did nothing to break America's reliance on oil. Americans today are consuming 2 million more barrels of oil a day than they did in 1989. "I was hoping for a huge shift in philosophy afterwards," says Riki Ott, a biologist and fisherman from the sound who wrote a 2008 book on the spill entitled *Not One Drop.* "But it hasn't worked that way yet."

The notion that Alaska was unspoiled until the *Exxon Valdez* accident never fit with reality, though. Vast tracts of America's Arctic northwest are sparsely populated wilderness, true, but the state has been a petroleum producer since crude was discovered in south-central Alaska's Kenai Peninsula in 1957. Today, Alaska disgorges 5 million barrels of oil a day, second only to Texas in the U.S., and the Prudhoe Bay field on the state's North Slope—the source of the crude spilled by the *Exxon Valdez*—is the biggest in the country. Alaska is almost as much a petro-state as Saudi Arabia or Kuwait. Taxes and other proceeds from oil and natural-gas production generate 84% of government revenues. "In many ways, Alaska is oil," says state lawmaker Bryce Edgmon.

But Alaska is also America's "last frontier," and this leaves many of the state's residents conflicted: they revel in the wealth oil brings, but fear its environmental toll. It's a conflict that in many ways mirrors the world's current dependence on petroleum at a time when the burning of fossil fuels is putting the planet on a path to catastrophe. Indeed, Alaska is becoming a test case to determine how people choose between oil-driven prosperity and environmental health. The clock is ticking: the giant reservoir of crude beneath Prudhoe Bay is quickly being pumped dry. Alaska's oil production has declined 38% over the past decade, and there are concerns that the Trans-Alaska Pipeline, which now carries half as much oil as it did at its peak, might not be viable in the near future unless new supplies are brought online.

There's a lot more crude out there. An estimated 27 billion barrels of oil are believed to lie beneath the state's southwestern Bering Sea and the ice-choked Chukchi and Beaufort Seas off Alaska's North Slope. But are Americans willing

Yet as shocking as the accident was, especially for Alaskans whose livelihoods suffered, its long-term impact on the U.S. more than two decades later can seem all but invisible, like those last pockets of oil trapped beneath the beach. Although the Oil Pollution Act of 1990 passed in the accident's immediate wake led to local improvements in shipping crude—like a mandatory shift to double-hulled tankers—spills still occur in the U.S., most recently in a 2007 accident in the San Francisco Bay that released 58,000 gallons (220,000 liters) of crude. While the partial meltdown at the Three Mile Island power plant in 1979 halted the nuclear industry in the U.S.,

to pay the price to get it? Drilling offshore in these wild waters poses an environmental risk. A loose coalition—greens who fear for endangered species like the polar bear, fishermen who worry about what another major spill could do to their livelihood, Alaskan natives defending their traditional lifestyle—is fighting to keep offshore oil off-limits. It's a battle, fought from the tundra of the North Slope to the federal courts of Washington, for the future of the state—and with 13% of the world's remaining undiscovered oil believed to lie in Arctic regions, it's a battle that will likely be waged again and again in the decades ahead as the global economy moves from an era of abundant oil to one of relative scarcity. "We know from the legacy of the *Exxon Valdez* what's at stake here," says Rick Steiner, a marine conservationist with the University of Alaska. "The Arctic is going to be a very interesting place from now on in."

Oil on the Rocks

I'M FLYING OVER BRISTOL BAY IN SOUTH-central Alaska in a six-seat Piper Aztec E, and am trying very hard not to throw up. The wind buffeting our plane gusts at over 37 m.p.h. (60 km/h)—which pilot Theo Colson explains "is really nothing around here." Fed by the rich waters of the Bering Sea, Bristol Bay is the most valuable commercial fishery in the U.S., producing more than $2 billion annually in king crab, herring and salmon. Northern right whales and other rare marine mammals depend on the bay; passing over one stretch of coastline we see a herd of walruses a thousand strong. As we near our destination, a former Air Force base named Cold Bay, Colson points out the expanse of churning water that the U.S. Department of the Interior aims to lease for offshore oil-and-gas development. Like most people in the Bristol Bay area, Colson is a part-time fisherman and he worries that a spill, or just the impact of new oil-and-gas production infrastructure, could damage the fish. "Oil is the biggest concern in our minds," says Colson. "One weak link could bring this whole area down. I'm not an environmentalist, but I do give a s___ about the land."

Over 800 miles (1,300 km) away in the town of Barrow—the northernmost point in the U.S.—Edward Itta holds the same concerns, though he expresses them less scatologically. Itta is the mayor of the North Slope Borough, a 88,750-square-mile (142,000 sq km) stretch of tundra hard by the iceberg-laden Beaufort Sea. They've long welcomed oil development on the North Slope—the Prudhoe Bay field is 200 miles (320 km) east of Barrow—and revenue from fossil-fuel development has supplied what would otherwise be economically barren towns and villages with modern hospitals, SUVs and satellite TVs. But drilling offshore is another matter. The Inupiat natives, who make up most of the 8,000 people who live on the North Slope, still practice a traditional way of life that centers on semiannual hunts for bowhead whales. The ocean is their garden, the saying goes, and many Inupiat fear that putting clanging, dirty oil rigs

AN ANCIENT WAY OF LIFE *Caribou on the tundra; North Slope Borough Mayor Edward Itta wants to preserve native culture*

in the Chukchi and Beaufort Seas will drive away the whales and destroy what's left of their culture. "A risk to the whale is a risk to us," says the soft-spoken Itta. "This has been too much, too soon, too fast."

The Inupiat and the fishermen of Bristol Bay fear offshore oil development would inevitably lead to a spill, and that cleaning it up would be virtually impossible. They remember the assurances that Exxon gave to the people of Prince William Sound that such a thing was unlikely to happen, and they remember the sluggish, confused cleanup effort, the years of bad fishing returns and the nightmarish images of oil-coated beaches. Cleaning up a spill is harder in cold water—the oil disperses much more slowly—and organizing a rapid response to a major accident in the remote Arctic would be like nothing the industry has faced. "I've been on icebreakers and I know the area," says Thomas Lohman, a lawyer

with the North Slope Borough's Department of Wildlife Management. "No one can assure me that you can properly armor offshore facilities there to make them work."

To Shell, the multinational oil company that has taken the lead on exploring Alaska's offshore territories, such fears are overblown. Shell officials point to the many exploratory wells that have already been drilled in the Beaufort and Chukchi Seas without incident, and the company's success in keeping discharges in its offshore facilities in the Gulf of Mexico to a minimum, even during Hurricane Katrina. Shell acknowledges that a full-scale operation in the Arctic won't be risk-free, but the company has been drilling in Alaska's Cook Inlet for years without a catastrophe. "It's different than the Arctic, but it's every bit as challenging," says Peter Slaiby, the general manager of Shell Alaska. "When we go up there we'll be ready to address any oil spill from the moment we're on the ground."

Environmentalists, though, worry that the fragile Arctic and subarctic environments could be damaged even if no oil is ever spilled. The polar bear, now listed as threatened under the U.S. Endangered Species Act, roams the sea ice that forms each winter on the Beaufort and Chukchi Seas, and bear populations are shrinking due to the impact of global warming on their habitat. The roads and pipelines and pumping stations that would inevitably accompany offshore oil development could put even more

PAUL FUSCO—MAGNUM PHOTOS

BLACK PLAGUE
Workers clutch wildlife killed by the 1989 spill

pressure on the animals. "The sea ice is already being hammered by global warming," says Margaret Williams, the managing director of the Bering Sea and Kamchatka program for the WWF. "If you explore for oil and natural gas, and add the disturbance of infrastructure, the Arctic is being hit with a triple whammy."

These fears are being acknowledged. In April 2009, a U.S. court threw out a plan put forward by the Bush Administration to develop Alaska's offshore oil and gas on the grounds that the Department of the Interior—charged with regulating fossil-fuel development—had failed to properly consider the environmental sensitivity of the areas. Ken Salazar, President Barack Obama's Interior Secretary, has suspended new offshore leases, and seemed receptive to local concerns when he recently visited the Bristol Bay area. "Just Salazar coming here spoke volumes, and gave us hope that our voices will be heard," says Ralph Anderson, the head of the Bristol Bay Native Association.

In the Balance

IN THE LONG RUN, THE BERING, BEAUFORT and Chukchi Seas will be at increasing risk for a simple reason: economics. Even at the lower end of estimates, untapped oil deposits off Alaska's coast could be worth more than $1 trillion. The International Energy Association predicts that, barring major policy changes, global demand for oil will rise from 85 million barrels a day to 106 million barrels a day in 2030. That oil will need to come from somewhere, and in the U.S. that somewhere is likely to include Alaska. America can choose to forgo developing the state's offshore resources—although the public outcry over high gas prices in 2008 showed how politically difficult that will be—but then it will just need to buy its oil from somewhere else, where environmental regulations might be weaker. "Offshore is needed to get the U.S. off foreign oil," says Marilyn Crockett, the executive director of the Alaska Oil and Gas Association. "We should be doing everything we can to reduce that dependence." Says Itta, the North Slope Borough mayor: "I do fear that a choice might be inevitable, and I'm not sure what the right one is. It's the kind of choice that wakes you up at 3:30 in the morning and you can't get back to sleep. How the hell do you balance it?"

It's a troubling question to ponder on a flawless afternoon as I sail past the crumbling glaciers of Prince William Sound, looking for traces of an accident that occurred 20 years ago. The taint of the *Exxon Valdez* has largely been dispersed. The sound, and the animals and people who live here, have recovered. Still, there's a lingering sense that paradise has been forever stained—and within that loss is a growing understanding that as long as we rely on oil, we'll never be free of the shadow of the *Exxon Valdez*. Riki Ott, the Prince William Sound biologist, fisherman and author, has traveled around the U.S. for the past few years as a public speaker, telling anyone who'll listen about how her home was harmed by the spill. She still holds out hope that the accident can change people's attitudes. She hopes, even, that a shift is already under way. "When I talk to people, they're not saying that they need more oil," Ott says. "They want a sustainable future for themselves and their kids." We're a long way from such a future. But it's one worth hoping for. ∎

A Good Year

We idolize the Paris uprising and not the fall of communism. That should change

BY MARTIN IVENS

IN THE VERY MONTH that he became Britain's Prime Minister, Gordon Brown published a book on political courage. Among his eight profiles were men and women who had struggled against the Nazis, South African apartheid and racial injustice in the U.S. Brown wrote that these heroes "have done more than almost any other men or women I can think of to advance the great causes of our times."

But one great cause was missing: anticommunism. So no room for Andrei Sakharov, Nien Cheng, Vaclav Havel or Pope John Paul II. Brown isn't the only member of the governing élite to identify more with the '60s than with the fall of the Wall. The 1968 generation, of which the Prime Minister was a member as a precocious Edinburgh student, just doesn't dig 1989.

The celebrations in the West of the greatest explosion of political freedom in our lifetimes, the collapse of the hideous ideology of communism, will be muted. Sure, there will be books, and state television companies will dutifully broadcast box-ticking documentaries. But the political class does not seem unduly moved by the date.

Compare and contrast. In 2008, France enjoyed an orgy of '68 retrospectives in print and on TV. Op-Ed columns across the U.S. groaned with reflections on youth rebellion by aging hipsters. In Britain the BBC's airwaves were jammed with excited chatter about what you wore to the great anti–Vietnam War demonstration in London's Grosvenor Square.

The personal is political, wrote the New York feminist Carol Hanisch in an influential essay. The Me generation took her all too literally. All those radical *soixante-huitards* subsequently enjoyed a long march through the institutions of the establishment, seizing control of the culture. Eventually they got to commission programs about themselves and their more outrageous and talkative friends. They could relive the heady days of their youth. To adapt Wordsworth on the French Revolution: Bliss was it in that dawn to be alive, but to look back on it all later, armed with a fat production budget, was very heaven.

To these guys—they usually are men—1989 happened over there, in the East, a place of which '68ers know little and care less. But the events of 1968 were here, spilling onto the streets of Paris, Chicago, Berlin, Rome and dozy London. For many, too, the '60s are still sexy and 1989 is, well, just worthy. The music and clothes were definitely better in 1968. Even kids today can get a kick out of the Rolling Stones' "Street Fighting Man." But bland, boppy singers like Kylie Minogue or the plastic soul of the Fine Young Cannibals? Forget it.

Thanks to the '68 generation, Western youth by 1989 had all manner of personal freedoms just as capitalism was entering upon one of its turbocharged moments. *Les événements* in Paris had begun over the right to entertain girlfriends overnight on campus, long before they matured into an assault on President De Gaulle. The students threw rocks to get their rocks off. East Germans in 1989 didn't want for sex—communist societies provided abortion on demand—but there were other kinds of freedom that mattered to them too.

The harsh truth may also be that not enough people died in that final struggle in the East to make Westerners commemorate its heroes as they should. In its heyday, communism concealed its monstrous crimes rather well from those who didn't want to know the truth. The Oscar-winning film *The Lives of Others* was such a hit because it came as a genuine surprise to many educated Western viewers that the Stasi in East Germany was so oppressive.

Then the end came with a peaceful rush. Except at Tiananmen Square and in Romania, the streets didn't run with the blood of democratic martyrs. The demonstrators in Leipzig, Prague and a score of other cities weren't to know that the authorities would balk at the last moment at mowing them down in a hail of bullets. Their courage was extraordinary, but complacent Westerners just don't appreciate the risks they had been running for decades, blighting their job prospects, putting their children's places in universities at stake. The quiet heroes of this revolution were to be in found in churches, peace groups, factories and intellectual seminars. Real bravery is hard work and unglamorous, the sort of struggle that is harder to maintain than throwing stones at police in Chicago and London.

Still, don't despair. One day the torch will pass from the '68ers. That's the good thing about being an '89er; our time will come. ∎

Ivens is deputy editor of Britain's Sunday Times